~ March 2020 ~

To Steve

I mow, ...
enjoy this.

It was written by our
neighbor, Fred Dickey who
was a columnist for the
San Diego Union Tribune.

There is a story in here
about Gracie and Balto also.

Love you Both so much!
XO   XO

Buffy #2? #3?
(I can never remember
what # I am!)

Fred Dickey—Career Achievement Award, 2017,
Northern Illinois University:
"For distinguished service to the journalism profession."

Available through book stores or on Amazon: print, or Kindle E-book.

For comments or reprint permission,
contact Fred Dickey at freddickey7@gmail.com

Published by Public Interest Media
Shorebird30@gmail.com

Cover artwork by Lionel Talaro, La Mesa, Calif.
Interior design by Delaney-Designs.com

ISBN: Print: 978-0-692-98915-9
E-Book: 978-0-692-98916-6

STORIES *With* FACES

The tightrope lives of next-door people

FRED DICKEY

For the fair Kathy: loving wife, smart partner, accomplished scientist, exasperating editor, good buddy, and amazingly tolerant human.

Order of Appearance

A businessman whose product is himself

Placido Camacho

This businessman is old school. He believes a man should be dignified, gentlemanly, and as well dressed as his job allows. To abide by that rule, he puts on his three-piece suit, carefully knots his tie and combs his hair and then checks the mirror a final time. He has his pride and an image to maintain. He is proud to tell you how important his work is.

He gets in his vehicle and drives from Oceanside, Calif. to his job site in Encinitas. The staff sees him strolling across the parking lot and they know a wide range of things will be taken care of.

He is Placido Camacho, a small man of 64 made taller with a straight back and uplifted face. His home is a rented room with the bathroom down the hall. His vehicle is a small 1997 Isuzu pickup. English is a rock-strewn mountain he struggles to climb every day.

He doesn't worry about the CIA, about global warming, or where the Chargers will play. He worries that the old truck will start when he turns the key.

His professional duties are discharged at the fast-food restaurant, El Pollo Loco, where his versatility is both prized and praised. He busses tables, cleans restrooms, sweeps floors and chops vegetables. He also fills in on the register; not just anyone does that. For 13 years, he has done whatever is needed, and never has to be asked twice.

Placido's employment earns him $11.50 per hour, but he doesn't complain, because he'd probably do it for less.

But those are just tasks. His real work—his *profesion*, as he calls it—is serving customers. He brings food to tables and offers a smile as a free "side." He is the closest you will find to a fast-food maitre d'.

He's also a teacher, but more on that in a minute.

He passes out the Mexican cinnamon pastry, *churro*, to children who eat their meals, and even if they don't; or if they're well behaved, or even if they're not. It's a bluff. Even a half-eaten meal is rewarded. He's an easy mark with the churros.

"I think about my own kids, and I feel like it's my kids. I want to make sure they eat. I talk to the kid. I'm all like, 'Okay, you have to eat your food. I have a surprise at the end when you finish your food. Then you can show me the plate."

He even gives me a churro just because I'm sitting there: an older customer who is reasonably well behaved and who also cleaned his plate, even though he probably shouldn't have. That's how I met him—through a churro, a multicultural sign of goodwill.

* * *

Placido was born in rural Oaxaca, Mexico, one of 11 children of a fisherman. The house he was raised in was one large room—just one. The kitchen and toilet were outside. He was only able to complete the fourth grade.

The only amelioration to those struggles was the presence of even poorer families in the neighborhood. Count your blessings.

When he started his own family, which grew to six children, they lived in relative largess in three rooms with an inside kitchen. The toilet, though, stayed outside.

He worked as a mechanic to support his family. "I used to work Monday to Friday," he says, "and then on the weekends I used to sell books."

Were you able to earn enough to keep food on the table?

"It was very hard; we had beans and eggs. We ate meat at least once a week."

He came north at age 51 to join some of his children who preceded him. His wife remains in Oaxaca. His hope is that she can "get her papers together" and join him. In his circumstance, a split family is not unusual.

His daughter was working at El Pollo Loco when he arrived, so he used that connection to get hired. He's never left.

He says his zeal for a life of service started 20 years ago when he discovered his spiritual side.

"I start reading the Bible and I feel like I become more like a gentleman. It make me become a better person than the person that I was before."

Placido is not a man with great entertainment demands. He says, "When I'm not at work, I like to sing and play with my guitar. I sing for God, and I also go to church."

The best part of his day is making kids happy. Maybe it goes back to the poverty of Oaxaca when churros were dear.

"A lot of the mothers that comes with the kids, and they go like, 'Oh, Placido, thank you so much. My kids are like grown up and healthy because you make them eat when we used to come here.'"

Bella Tijero, his assistant manager, says that if Placido has a day off, she's seen children who come to the restaurant expecting to see him, but then break into tears.

Moist eyes also happen to Placido when he describes a mother who comes into the restaurant with her special-needs child on Saturdays. The child looks forward to seeing him, and he the child. As he describes the hug he receives, his voice catches, and he pauses and lowers his face as though to say grown men aren't supposed to show that emotion.

Yeah, Placido, I think they should, for the right purpose. It's a manly thing.

* * *

Placido is not a simple man, because there is no such thing. Rather, he is a poor man and a proud man. Those are not complementary, but neither are they contradictory.

If I were teaching a career-preparation course in college, I would certainly bring into class the CEOs, the CFOs, and all those other "C" dudes. But I'd also bring in Placido to tell students things about the meaning of work that aren't in the syllabus.

Placido's story is as modest as he. It's about the pleasure of giving a churro to a child. It's about a humble man being a rich man.

San Diego Union-Tribune, March 13, 2017

Detective Mo retraces a murderer's steps

Mo Parga

Mo Parga, 53, is a colorful San Diego P.D. detective. In her 32 years as a street cop, from horse patrol to homicide, this is the case most stark in her memory, and for which she was given an award.

It is Sunday morning, Feb. 3, 2002 on Mountain Pass Road in the Sabre Springs area of San Diego near Poway.

Detective Mo Parga parks her unmarked car amidst a scattering of squad cars along the clean, quiet street. All she knows is that a 7-year-old girl disappeared from her bed late Friday night or very early Saturday morning.

Mo has been summoned to join the search because an initial sweep of the neighborhood and nearby canyons has not found Danielle Nicole Van Dam. It quickly escalates from "missing juvenile" to suspected kidnapping. That has brought in Mo; kidnappings are part of her job.

Mo stands on the sidewalk in front of the very nice two-story home of Damon and Brenda Van Dam where they live with two young sons and Danielle.

The detective tries to think of Danielle without seeing her face, because she intuitively fears the little girl is dead. Working this case is going to be awful enough without being haunted by an image.

She hopes she's wrong, but 17 years as a cop have imprinted dark truths in her mind. Wishes play no part is solving a crime.

Little girls don't wander off, and when they "run away from home" in a pout, it's to hide under their bed until they get hungry.

No, if she returns home, it'll be a miracle. Much more likely, when she's found, it'll be a tragedy. Mo pushes those thoughts from her mind. She knows other detectives are trying to push away the same fear.

* * *

Mo is doing a routine neighborhood canvass and finds herself in front of a house two doors from the Van Dams. She will soon learn it belongs to David Westerfield, a successful work-at-home engineer of 49, a bachelor who keeps to himself.

All she knows at the moment is that the resident is a man who lives alone and is not home. Neighbors say he is known as "Desert Dave" for his frequent camping trips to the desert.

She admires Westerfield's putting-green lawn with its clipped shrubs and swept walks. She finds it especially attractive because out where she lives in East County, grass can be considered frivolous. Horses prefer weeds.

She also notices a garden hose stretched across his lawn to the curb and back. It is just lying there.

Mo studies it, and thinks—A fussy gardener would never do this because it will turn the underneath grass yellow. Why the rush?

The wheels whirr in her head like fruit in the window of a slot machine. When they stop, they leave no doubt in her mind—

It's him. The guy who was in too big a hurry to rewind his hose—he's our guy. She doesn't yet know his name, but she's convinced he's the man who took the little girl.

It's a presumption that other cops might roll their eyes at, but it isn't a wild guess, at least not to her. It's based on keen observation and a long time spent figuring out how guilty people act. Yes, it's a form of profiling, and is certainly a rush to judgment.

Walking back to the command post, she strides into the murmuring group of brass and detectives trying to sort out how to tackle the mystery (Mo is not a shy woman). She points to the hose and explains her rationale.

"One says, 'Aw, come on, Mo. You're not going to solve this case over a stupid garden hose.' "

She answers, "I'm just telling you, we need to look at this guy. He did something."

Not only that, she tells them the neighbors have said that Westerfield went away for the weekend on Saturday morning in his motor home. How convenient. And that doesn't remove him from the crime scene or the timeline.

That's a lot of theory for connect-the-dots investigators to absorb all of a sudden, and here's Mo jumping dots like a grasshopper. However, they don't ridicule her ideas.

You can tease Mo, but don't roll your eyes when she's talking to you. And as she argues, they slowly come around, very tentatively. They have nothing better working at the moment, so Lt. Jim Collins, the officer in charge, tells Mo to go ahead and work her theory.

Mo and her partner, Johnny Keene, stake out the Westerfield house until 3 a.m. Monday, then thick fog rolls in and they leave. Westerfield comes home at 8:45 that morning where he is met by other detectives.

Mo and Keene are summoned and arrive at 9 a.m. Westerfield is standing in the driveway. He quickly singles her out and tries to build a rapport. She sees him sweating profusely which she considers tell-tale because it's a frigid morning.

Trying to put him at ease, she tells him all the homes in the area are going to be examined, and she'd really appreciate seeing his. He invites her into the house and Keene follows.

"I'm not about to go in there alone."

Inside, Keene fades into the background and spends his time checking things out. Westerfield seems to be "coming on" to Mo and offers to fix her lunch, which she declines.

"I go upstairs, and he shows us his bedroom. He's a show-off, bragging about all his stuff.

"I go into his bathroom, and when I go to the window and look out, I can see the Van Dam house, and there is an impression in the screen. I fit my face into the impression, and it looks right down and across to where Danielle would play."

Are you being coy with him?

"Yeah, I am—'Wow, this is a really beautiful house.'—He's interacting with me, I'm interacting back. I don't want him to all of a sudden decide, 'OK, get out of my house.'

"On the kitchen counter, there is a cut out catalog picture of a child's bed. I'm thinking, Wow! This is spooky—

"I had gone into Danielle's room to get hair from her brush yesterday.

"She had a canopy bed—No, 'has.' I don't want to think that way—It's white and pink, and this picture on his counter is very similar to her bed....So, why would a middle-age bachelor have that? He's the guy, definitely. He's the guy.

"Westerfield is divorced, and he says to me that I look like his ex-wife, and that may be why he's comfortable talking to me. I'll take it."

Do you think Westerfield believes he can manipulate you?

"He's a very intelligent man. He's a sick individual, but he's not stupid. He just thinks I am."

And you want him to think that, right?

"Yeah, oh, yeah."

She notices he has a Toyota 4Runner in the garage. It's been freshly cleaned inside and out. Mo's immediate hunch is that he used it to transport Danielle to his motor home which he keeps some distance away.

* * *

It's now Monday afternoon, and Mo breaks away and rejoins the other investigators. As they talk, the others come around to her point of view, one by one. Westerfield's name is now in bold face. They ask her to return and keep him talking while they seek search warrants.

She goes back and sits with Westerfield for several hours to buy time. Keene is still poking around taking notes, but Westerfield tends to forget he's there. He becomes part of the furniture, which is the idea. She has to sit and try to make small talk with a man she is convinced is a child killer.

At one point, he again seems to be coming on to her. He invites her to dinner. She's thinking—Yeah, that's what I need, a boyfriend who kills children.

"So I said, no, we're not going to go out and have dinner."

Mo wants to earn Westerfield's trust so maybe he'll confess or blurt out what he did. It sometimes happens that way.

She wants him to believe her when she says, "I want you to know that whatever happens, I'll be there and make sure everything is done right." She lies with a straight face. "Just show me where Danielle is, if you know."

He asks if he's under arrest. "No you're not, David. This little girl is missing, and we have to find her." She tells him other neighbors are being interviewed, including the parents.

Mo is sympathetic. She is his new friend. "I know this is really putting you out. You're probably tired from driving back from—I forget, where were you?"

She finally asks him to take a polygraph exam, downplaying it by saying others are doing it, and it just helps investigators clear people.

He agrees, so they drive to the northeastern police station on Salmon River Road. She waits while he takes the test. Later, when he's told he failed, he says, "I don't know why."

Mo's job is done for the day and Westerfield says he's hungry and is going home for dinner. He then drives back to his house to find detectives waiting to serve him with a search warrant. It was obtained while he was occupied by Mo's "harmless" conversation.

It can't have helped his appetite.

Westerfield's denials quickly collapse. Investigators find Danielle's blood or hair evidence in his house, the Toyota, and the motor home.

He is arrested on Feb. 22, 2002, three days before his 50th birthday. Danielle's body is found in rural East County near Sycuan casino five days later.

* * *

Retired Capt. Jim Collins (then lieutenant) was in charge of the investigation. This is how he sorts out the scenario of the abduction.

Westerfield had seen Brenda and her girl friends in a local bar the previous Friday night (Jan. 25). Then, by happenstance, she and Danielle went to his house on Wednesday, five days later, to sell him Girl Scout cookies.

He invited them in and asked her why she hadn't introduced him to her girl friends at the bar. During the conversation in his home (and probably his probing) she happened to say she and her friends would probably be at the same bar the coming Friday (Feb. 1) for a going-away party, provided she could get a baby sitter for Danielle, because Damon and the boys would be out of town.

Consequently, when Westerfield observed Brenda and her friends at the bar on Friday night, he soon left, presumably to prepare Danielle's abduction. We can only guess what would have been the fate of a babysitter had she been there.

However, Damon and the two boys had cancelled their trip, and there was no babysitter. That Westerfield did not awaken the sleeping three, was able to find the right bedroom, alert the dog, or cause an outcry by Danielle as he swept her away, is an ugly chain of improbable circumstances.

(We can only marvel at the force of the dreadful compulsion that drove him to take such a foolish chance.)

So, not realizing Damon and the boys were all at home, Westerfield crept through an open side-yard door, through an unlocked garage door, and up the stairs to Danielle's room with cat-burglar stealth.

He then carried her small sleeping (or muffled) body back to his home. Hours later, he put her in the cargo area of his Toyota and drove to his motor home to which he transferred Danielle, living or dead. He then returned to the house where he hastily filled the vehicle's water reservoir—Remember the hose in the yard?—and then drove away. Danielle was not discovered missing until around 9 Saturday morning.

Mo looks back on the case with regret that the Westerfield defense chose to portray the Van Dams as bad parents, which the press repeated. Did I say "regret"? No, "anger."

She recalls how horrible she felt asking Brenda to lead her to the garage where Mo would look for evidence; the hard-to-miss implication was that the parents might become suspects.

"That was heart wrenching. They were loving parents. Brenda was a mess. Can you imagine: I'm going into your house, your child's missing, and I'm asking you where the duct tape and zip ties are, indicating that this is what might have happened to your child, and you did it?"

* * *

Would Westerfield have been caught without Mo's educated guess?...Bet on it. A little girl murdered? Cops are parents, and have teeth that don't let go of child-killing cases. And Westerfield, as smart as he may have thought he was, didn't realize that a hose and rag can't erase all forensic evidence.

As Mo testified at the trial, she looked over at Westerfield sitting at the defense table to see him smiling at her. She didn't smile back. Smiling was no longer a part of her job description.

He was convicted of Danielle's abduction and murder, and on August 21, 2002 was sentenced to death, and now reposes on death row.

Westerfield never had the chance to take Mo to that dinner he proposed, although she says she'd happily serve him his last meal.

We will probably never know, but maybe Danielle was not the only one. We don't want to think about that.

* * *

In August 2018, Mo Parga will retire and, over time, settle into being Mrs. Maura Mekenas-Parga. Her horses out in East County will benefit from many more cubes of sugar, but they'll also have to carry her around those hills a lot more.

Thus will exit this street cop who can get all squint-eyed and grim faced, but I've also seen her shed a tear for a victim.

But help is on the way.

In a future police academy class, maybe even the current one, there is a quipy, saucy gal who gives as well as she gets, and is liked as one of the guys. The difference is that today's "guys" are not the guys they used to be.

Mo redux. The baton will pass.

San Diego, Union-Tribune, May 1, 2017

A sad girl loses her 'best friend'

Gracie and Balto

Gracie Howard is losing her first best friend. A little girl is learning that loss is part of life: Love that is clasped to the heart is destined to be torn away. Always. Always.

It is just the way it is, and we all have to learn that. It can be hard to deal with, but there's a sweetness to it because to have loved at all is the greatest human achievement.

* * *

This is the last day of Balto's life. And, on balance, his dog's life has been a lucky one, discounting a rocky start. He is a male husky who somehow ended up on the streets of Baja, Mexico about 13 years ago as a homeless stray.

Balto is lying flat on a pad in the family room of a Cardiff, Calif. home this morning, sound asleep. He's about 50 pounds, but looks 80 with his long, thick coat. He's a gentle dog that rarely barks and has none of the aggressive or fearful behavior that street dogs often adopt in survival mode.

The veterinarian will arrive in a few minutes. The family waits in a limbo of funk, tip-toeing quietly around Balto.

Gracie is a blond Norman Rockwell girl of 8. She sits on a nearby couch with her legs curled up and is holding a comfort blanket and stuffed dog of—right, a husky. She is quietly doing what they used to call "keening"; not quite crying, but softly grieving with tears coursing down her cheeks. She swipes at them and talks very grown-up about her old friend Balto.

"Today is the day my dog is going to get put down. He's just getting older and older by the day, and we think it'll be good because he's kind of suffering, so today we're going to put him down."

When Balto decides to rise, he has to be helped to his feet, then he wanders off, but only for a short distance. He walks like Charlie Chaplin portraying a drunk, bumping into walls, furniture and spilling his water. He tires quickly and returns to his pad.

Gracie says, "At first, I said I want to go to school today, but I didn't really want to do that. So I said, 'Mom, I changed my mind,' and I ran over to her and told her, 'I want to stay at my house, and be there for this sad occasion.'"

Out of the mouth of a third-grader.

She describes her love affair with this animal that has always been a part of her life—the way he would prance on his paws and "tap dance"; how he would all of a sudden get "really hyper" and start tearing around the yard in what she called "having a bee in his bonnet."

The memories are just too sad, and Gracie returns to being a small girl. She begins to cry, and then talks in those gulps between sobs that we remember from our own childhoods.

"I'm bummed out, but I am happy. I'm happy he's going to be in heaven. He won't be here. He'll be playing with tennis balls. He'll be eating treats, and he'll be playing with toys like he always used to."

Gracie leaves the couch and lies down next to the resting dog, hugs him, kisses his ear, then returns.

Did your parents ask if you thought he should be put down?

"No," she says, "but I'm happy because I'd say to let him live longer. But then we'd make him feel worse, because then he'd be feeling much badder right now. So I think it's good to just let him go."

Gracie says, "I've learned that things don't always go the way you've planned. Sometimes people die, but that doesn't mean they're away from you. They still haven't left your heart. They'll always live with you. Even though they might get buried, we'll always remember them."

That's verbatim, I swear.

Children can be amazing, mainly because we don't pay close attention to their small leaps of maturity. Then, they hit us with wisdom, and we wonder—Where did she learn that?

* * *

The veterinarian is here. She is Tracey Herman of Carlsbad, a friendly young woman who has known Balto well.

She chats a few minutes, then her technician, Kaitlin Parker, skillfully inserts an IV into Balto's paw and injects a sedative which will fully take effect in about 10 minutes.

As we know, she could give a painless shot that would be fatal almost instantly, but I suspect the sedative is mainly for the family, for them to slowly accept the reality of what is about to happen. Or, at the last minute, change their minds.

* * *

Mark and Melissa Howard, Gracie's parents, have a get-away place in Baja to which they travel occasionally. During one trip about 13 years ago, Melissa says they saw a stray on the street, one that looked particularly out of place, as though it had wandered out of the Alaska tundra and down to Mexico. It was a sick, starving husky with that breed's thick, long coat trying to avoid fatal over-heating in Mexico by lying in the surf.

Balto, as he was to become, was a dog in deep, deep trouble.

Melissa's eyes redden as she remembers. "He wouldn't have lasted probably another month. He had a terrible ear infection that you could smell from a distance. He walked sideways, from a neurological condition.

"You could hear the liquid in his head slosh when he'd move. He had an eye that was closed from a rock somebody had thrown at him. He was infested with ticks and fleas; just in really terrible shape."

The Howards arranged for Balto to be cared for, but on a later visit decided to bring him back here to "find a home for him."

Well, you already know what home she found. Balto joined other Mexican strays the Howards have adopted. Melissa says, smiling, "Balto was a very expensive 'free' dog."

Mark Twain's words come to mind: "If you pick up a starving dog and make him prosperous he will not bite you. This is the principal difference between a dog and man."

* * *

Tracey says Balto currently has several ailments, neurological, orthopedic, and some infection problems dating to his time in Mexico that have returned opportunistically. All together, he's a very sick dog.

Deciding a dog has suffered enough is a decision that will always leave the owner feeling guilty, but the degree of guilt depends on the certainty of the decision.

The vet says she suggests a "three of five" test for owners as a guideline. That is, when a dog that seems borderline can no longer do three of five things it loves, then, maybe, it's time. She mentions such things as playing with a ball, responding to the garage door, or not eating snacks, or others. If so, then maybe...

Personally, I think the honest question pet owners must ask themselves is: Am I keeping this animal alive for the pet or for myself?

* * *

It's time. Tracey efficiently inserts a needle into the IV and injects a pentobarbital cocktail called Euthasol which stops the heart almost instantly.

It's done.

As the body of what once was beloved Balto lies on its pad awaiting removal, Gracie turns to her mother's arms and opens her emotions to broken-heart sobs.

Gracie will soon dry her tears, and time will fade her pain, leaving her a little more grown-up. Balto will become storied in her memory, and will come alive as a cute tale she someday can tell her own children of the big dog from Mexico that could tap dance.

Life, lost and found.

San Diego Union-Tribune, December 28, 2015

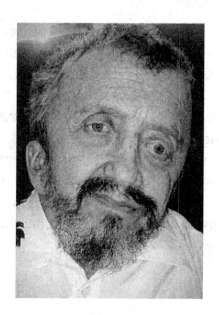

Dale Akiki

There are episodes in any city's history from which those involved will scurry away like a bridal party in a rainstorm. And if certain of San Diego's legal establishment of past years had their way, the case of Dale Akiki would be misfiled deep in cobwebbed archives. Our system tormented Akiki as cruelly as could any hooded Tudor executioner.

Dale Akiki, the man who endured that abuse, survived and sits in front of me in his modest Mira Mesa condo prepared to talk about those black days.

In 1988 Akiki says he started attending the large Faith Chapel church in Spring Valley. When the church was seeking volunteers, he offered to serve in the nursery school.

According to Akiki's lead counsel, Kate Coyne, after about a year, some parents started to protest, saying his looks were disturbing their children. The head of the Sunday school investigated and said she found no fault with Akiki and said the children loved him.

Coyne says events heated up when a mother started questioning her daughter in an "intensely suggestive manner" until sexual abuse accusations were forthcoming. The mother then went to the pastor who called the sheriff's office. The sheriff and the church sent inquiry letters to parents, and then the hysteria started to mushroom, Coyne says, and Akiki was asked to leave the church.

For two years authorities investigated the charges. In the meantime, Akiki met and married Sharon Bulger, who had also attended the church. His life returned to normal until 21 years ago today, May 10, 1991. On that day he was arrested while stepping off a city bus on his way home from work. He was carrying a bag of aluminum cans he regularly collected for his wife's spending money.

Of complete shock to him, he was charged with child abuse and kidnapping. The charges reached 52 counts by the time of the trial.

The result? Akiki found himself facing a lifetime in prison.

This is tough for him to relive, but he does not flinch from the memories. He's a soft-spoken, devout man of 54 with the moral strength that allowed him to climb some steep hills in his life. He carries a shunt inside his skull to ease migrane pressures on the brain. Even worse, he was born with a rare genetic disorder called Noonan's syndrome. It caused him to be small and slight, and with a noticeable limp and facial features irregular enough to get startled glances from strangers. Even, perhaps, enough to scare small children.

He is at ease with his debility and appearance. In a strong baritone voice that belies his size, he says, "There's nothing I can do about it, so I accept it, and trust other people to accept me on the type of person I am. I try to be a good friend and kind to all people."

After the arrest, he was forced to resign his job as a computer assistant for the Navy. He was held without bail for 30 months in the old downtown jail while awaiting trial and during it. Over that time, he was repeatedly denied bail because the court considered him a flight risk. He recalls one judge saying, "Well, if the other judges denied bail, I will too."

Once delivered to the jail, he was placed in protective custody. However, in any jail, "protective" is an iffy promise, and an accused child molester is a rabbit with no thicket to hide in.

The old downtown jail. Think dark, think shadowy, think cold stone and rusted steel, think hollow echoes of shouted anguish and angry taunts.

Akiki says he quickly learned there were bad guys in cells just yards from his who would have played with him like a doll.

"I got threats. Guys were threatening to kill me. I had things thrown at me when I went to the showers. It was a nightmare. I just closed my mind and day-dreamed that one day I would wake up and turn over in bed, and there would be my wife."

He recalls how those days in jail dragged and his spirits flagged. He sought comfort from his faith, but depression had a voice, too, and its whisper was low and coaxing.

"I always thought it they found me guilty I would've done something to myself. There's no way I was going to prison for something I didn't do."

That's suicide he's talking about.

Help in jail came from an unexpected source. Two southeast San Diego gang-bangers put the word out that if anyone messed with Akiki they would answer to them. Slowly over the months, the jail population rallied to Akiki's defense. It is a phenomenon of that culture to be protective of whomever they consider inno-cent and defenseless—their own victims excepted, of course.

He was also heartened by groups of faithful supporters who frequently gathered outside the jail for candlelight vigils and chanted for his freedom. His Navy co-workers turned out in force.

"I couldn't see, but I could hear them," he remembers. "Those people out there helped keep me going."

The case finally came to trial in 1993 and lasted seven and one-half months, and heard from 170 witnesses. It remains the longest trial in San Diego history.

Prosecutors alleged multiple sex acts against the children, and claimed they had "dozens and dozens" of children who would testify, according to Akiki's co-counsel, Susan Clemens, but they only called nine to the stand. The children were about three and four when the events supposedly occurred, and six to eight when they testified. Among other wildly bizarre things, they told the court that Akiki had killed a giraffe and an elephant in their presence and sacrificed a child and drank its blood in the nursery.

What the charges boiled down to was a twisted doctrine called "ritual sexual abuse" that gained a following back in that day: in effect, modern-day witchcraft.

I am not making this up. I wish I were.

When testimony ended in November 1993, the jury took only seven hours to return a not-guilty verdict. Akiki wept as the clerk's words told him he was finally going home.

Later, jurors were withering in their denunciation of every aspect of the state's case and anyone associated with it. The county grand jury later joined the chorus.

When he was released to cheers and news coverage, Akiki was driven home in style in a stretch limousine. It was paid for by 20 deputies at the jail.

He reached out for his former life. He got his Navy job back. His and Sharon's lives settled down uneventfully. They renewed their marriage vows on their fifth anniversary.

"We missed the second, third and fourth anniversaries," he says, "so we wanted to start fresh."

After the acquittal, he sued and won $2 million from the county, the church and therapists for what they had taken from him.

District Attorney Ed Miller was soundly voted out of office, largely as an outgrowth of this case. The chief prosecutor of the case, Mary Avery, was transferred, and eventually left the DA's staff.

His lawyers, Coyne and Clemens, were named California Public Defenders of the Year in 1994. Akiki says he still regards them as family.

Today, gray is spreading across his hair as Dale Akiki looks forward to retirement in September. The anticipation is muted by the loss of Sharon who died of an embolism in 2009 at age 45. Remarriage is not on his mind. "Sharon was my princess," he says of the woman who stood by him steadfastly. "I could never replace what she meant to me. She is still in my heart."

In the ensuing two decades, the church has not contacted him with an apology, regrets or even an offer for prayers. Neither have any of the children, now grown, attempted to talk to him. And if one did?

"I would say 'I didn't do anything to you, and you know I didn't, so why did you say those things?' "

The early '90s were a time when child sexual predation was coming to the fore of public awareness. That caused a surge of targeting those who had abused children for years with relative impunity. But rightness of the cause aside, there is a difference between zeal and zealotry, just as there is between love and jealousy. Always close behind the reformer is the man with the guillotine.

Looking back, who was at fault? Who caused this vile thing to happen to such a gentle man? The answer is elusive. Was it the children's parents who egged them on? Was it therapists and activists who needed a poster boy to pin their cause on? Was it the DA's office, hell-bent on getting a conviction? Was it the judges who could have thrown the case out, or who could at least have granted bail?

Maybe it was nobody. But if it was nobody, then it was everybody. And that's what's frightening, because that means it could happen again.

San Diego Union-Tribune, May 12, 2012

School killer looks back with remorse

He's not a kid anymore, he's a full-grown man. He's not five-four anymore, he's six-four. And now, he seems at peace with himself. Time, it seems, is not only a balm for victims, but also for those who victimize them.

He's a pleasant fellow with a quick smile and friendly greeting. But he's also a killer. You have to shake your head, both at the wonder of it, and the shame of it.

He's Charles Andrew "Andy" Williams. He was the child-like gunman, age 15 by one month,

Andy Williams

who killed two students and wounded 13 others on March 5, 2001 at Santana High School in the middle- to lower-middle-class San Diego suburb of Santee.

Now, 12 years later, he's willing to talk about that day and what led up to it: what he thought, what he did and why, every step of the way. It's all there, in his mind, and it will always be there.

He became a *cause celebre* of sorts as a symbol for bullied school children. However, prosecutors were neither impressed nor persuaded. Neither was the judge. When Williams pleaded guilty to first-degree murder, the court sentenced him to 50 years to life, which means he will be eligible for parole when others of his age are collecting Social Security.

He lives today at age 27 in protective custody in Ironwood State Prison. His neighborhood is the desolation of the desert 170 miles east of Riverside. The nearest town is Blythe. To get there, go to the moon and turn left at the second crater.

His cellmate is another felon. This is not a happy way to spend one's youth, nor middle age, nor old age. It might even be where he dies.

Sitting patiently for hours in a prison interview room, he is in his prison blues wearing horned rim glasses and a ready smile. He has avoided festooning his body with the crude tattoos commonly called "jailhouse art" that mark the bearer as a con as clearly as a sandwich board. He talks fast and softly, as though wanting to keep as many words in the air as possible before they fall on a listener's ears.

He has finished community college in prison and is close to becoming a journeyman bricklayer.

It's clear that prison guards trust, and sort of like him.

He does not deny his guilt, and agrees he should be punished. He does not plead for sympathy. He says he wants mainly to be understood. He doesn't say so, but I suspect he would also like for the public to see him as a nice guy, but he must know that will be a tough sell.

This is Andy Williams' story of what led to March 5, 2001 when a wayward boy turned into a kid killer.

* * *

Andy was a child of a divorce that broke apart his family when he was three years old. His mother and half-brother eventually moved away, and he stayed with his father in Brunswick, Md. Brunswick was basically a village, unthreatening for a young boy denied the comfort of a mother's presence.

He saw his mother infrequently, usually at Christmas, when he would travel to her distant home. He functioned suitably in school, finding approval because of his good behavior and open, joking personality. As he neared the end of grammar school, some disturbing traits developed, but he kept them hidden. If he felt depressed or abandoned by being separated from his mother, he also kept that hidden. His father, no one disputes, was supportive and loving.

When asked about his early childhood, Williams says, "To me, it was normal. It was cool for me; I had loving parents."

In December 1999, age13, he was uprooted and moved with his father to Twentynine Palms, Calif., a small city in the desert near Palm Springs, dominated by a nearby Marine base. It was a conservative environment housing many military retirees, including his grandfather, and was not a place where a kid could escape notice for getting into trouble.

Andy also benefited from the structure and values of his grandparents. In that community, he enjoyed the greatest success of his young life. He participated in eighth-grade activities, made friends, did his schoolwork, professed his Christian faith and was baptized.

But a few months in that nurturing place was all he would be given. His father, a laboratory-animal technician, accepted a job in San Diego at Balboa Naval Hospital. Before relocating, Andy was allowed to spend the summer of 2000 back in Maryland with friends. There, the discipline of Twentynine Palms disappeared like a desert rain, foreshadowing what lay ahead in Santee.

* * *

He deplaned at Lindbergh Field and traveled to his new apartment-home in Santee in the fall of 2000 to enroll at Santana High School for his freshman year. What 14-year-old Andy had kept concealed was that he had gotten into dope in Maryland that summer, and not for the first time. Even before his brief drug-free hiatus in Twentynine Palms, he has experimented with narcotics in Maryland.

"My friends and I started taking pills and going to harder stuff like cocaine. The first time I experienced those, I was 12 years old."

Williams recounts his first experience in Santee. "When I flew back from Maryland to Santee, I had some dope on me. I saw a church across the street that I was going to go to, and I thought, I got to get rid of this dope.

"However, the very first night I was home, I was smoking a cigarette on the lawn of our apartment complex, and this dude came up and he was, like, 'Hey, man, I'm out of drugs, and I got this freakin' pipe on me, and I got no dope.' I was, like, 'That's crazy. I got some dope, but no pipe. Let's smoke dope.' And through him I got to meet the guys who became my friends. The very first night I was there."

Andy quickly fell in with a group of boys who, in an earlier time, would have been called dead-end kids, who would be called losers by other teens, and problems by their teachers.

I asked why he didn't seek out the type of friends he had made in Twentynine Palms and adhere to the Christian standards he had embraced there. He simply says, "I don't know. I honestly don't know."

He had reached a crossroads in his young life, and he says he did wrestle with his devils, at least a little. "When I first went back to Maryland that summer, all my friends were using drugs, and I was, like, dude, I don't want to be around it. I remember praying a lot about it, saying, 'Lord, I'm going to hang out with these dudes now, but when I get to Santee I'm going to go to church again.'... I never did."

The three boys Andy became closest to were A.J. Gilbert, Shaun Turk and Josh Stevens, all about his age. The boys spent a lot of time at a nearby skateboard park and at each others' homes when responsible adults were absent.

Andy exploited a situation that makes working, single parents tear their hair: for many hours of each day, he was unsupervised and unrestrained from running free.

Williams says the boys drank alcohol and smoked pot at every opportunity. "A friend's mom had Lyme disease and she, like, she had all kinds of pain pills, and so we were just stealing them and eating opiates all the time."

He was asked if he has an addictive personality. "Yeah, yeah I do. But looking back, I think I felt I needed drugs to function. It was, like, if I didn't do something (drugs), it was a terrible day. In Maryland, it was just fun, but in Santee, it was like I had to. I was miserable. The people I was with, the environment...I got involved with the wrong people early on."

Andy at the time was a small boy for his age with a placating manner. As such, he was prey dished up warm for the bullies he ran with. Such people can scent weakness as easily as any hyena on the veldt. He was quickly singled out by his new friends as a foil for their aggression.

He says they punched and kicked him, stole his possessions, and even sprayed his pants legs with lighter fluid and set him afire. Beating up on Andy was fun and easy.

Did he ever fight back? "At first, but then I thought if someone comes up and socks me, I'm going to be hurt less if I just let it happen." Instead, he became a clown, hoping that amusing his companions would buy him a reprieve from the bullying. It didn't work. The mystery is why he kept coming back for more.

"I don't know. I thought these guys are cool, and I wanted to be cool.

I've always wished I was a little bit braver. It was just easier to (go along) than to, like, stand up on my own two feet and tell people what I was about."

At Santana, his schoolwork didn't just suffer, it collapsed. Constant skipping and ignored homework marked him as a dead-beat to other students and an exasperation to teachers.

Did your dad know you were hanging around with the wrong kids?

"Initially, no, but the more we were skipping school and the more people's parents would come and complain to him about stuff we were doing, he got the sense that I was probably in a bad crowd."

Was your rebellion about being with him rather than in Georgia with your mother?

"Uh, I wouldn't—I liked that I was with my dad. Like, it would have been cool to be with my mom, but I don't think I would have ever left my dad."

Did you tell your dad you needed to leave Santee?

"I never had the courage to tell him I was struggling. I didn't want to let him down. I had no idea what to do."

He says he was also bullied at Santana High School, but he was reminded that after the shooting no teacher, administrator or student at Santana High School said they ever saw him bullied.

He counters that bullying goes on all the time beneath the noses of teachers and principals. "At school, they would take my money. I'd have my backpack ripped off and thrown in the trashcan. In high school, if they see a kid not fighting back, they think he's an easy target. I was little and easy, I guess."

Was there anything in Santee or at Santana that could have made it different for you?

"Absolutely. There were some real cool Christians, like, I always wanted to be a part of, but I didn't want my friends seeing me like that."

Next into his life came Chris Reynolds, an adult sexual predator who Williams says lived in the same house as Josh Stevens and who turned Andy's mixed-up life into a maelstrom.

Williams says Reynolds was the one who would buy alcohol and provide drugs for the boys. And, yes, there were strings attached.

"He was abusing all of us."

What was he doing?

"He'd grab on us and try to kiss us and stuff. If he wanted to grab someone's butt, it was, like, whatever, dude."

Is that what he did, grab you?

"And he did some other stuff."

What?

"He would, he would, he would grab us and try to do stuff to us."

What did he do?

"He would try to masturbate us."

Did he do it to you?

"He did it to me one time."

"You don't want to talk about that, do you?

(Nervous laughter) "Naaah."

How did that contribute to March 5th?

"When something like that happens to you, if you're not willing to stop that, then you'll just roll over for anything. That was really hard for me to deal with. If I was…if I was…if I was okay with that, then what am I?"

You never told your dad?

"No, but he told me later he knew that no 28-year-old is going to hang out with a bunch of kids, but I had told him nothing ever happened."

(Christopher E. Reynolds, 40, is serving a 40-year prison sentence in Oklahoma for lewd misconduct. He was invited by mail to respond but did not. If one plans to commit a sex crime, Oklahoma is probably a good place to drive through without stopping.)

Not long before the shooting, Williams says he and Josh Stevens concocted a scheme to run away to Mexico. They, of course, bragged of their scheme to all their buddies. Later, as the date neared, Williams says Josh backed out. However, to save face, he spread the word that Andy was the one who had chickened out. As word spread, the ridicule-prone Andy became a laughing stock among his friends.

* * *

FRIDAY, MARCH 2, 2001

Finally, the pressure from his misbehavior started to ratchet up. Andy's father, probably in a state of great frustration, drove him to school that Friday to confront the guidance counselor.

"He chewed out the counselor, that when I skipped school it was the school's responsibility to inform him of it."

The reality was, the school would leave a message on the home recorder noting his absence, and Andy would run home and erase it before his father could hear it.

Later that day, Andy, still upset over the counselor encounter, showed up for a class, unprepared as usual. This time, though, he remembers the teacher unloading on him in front of the other students for a lack of effort.

"I didn't do the homework, but the teacher let loose on me: what an idiot I was, and I was like a terrible person. It was bad. I just sat there and took it." It surely was not the first time he'd been criticized in class, but for some reason, it scraped a nerve. Williams says that it also deepened his depression and strengthened a growing urge to commit suicide.

"I got out of class and I went and told my friends, 'This chick yelled at me for a half-hour. I sure wish someone would shoot her.'" He says it was a threat that he immediately dismissed with "ha-ha-ha." He now describes the incident as "a verbal, pointless teenage threat on crappy teachers."

However, when he got together with his buddies later, they teased him that he wouldn't carry through with his threats to shoot the teacher because he had backed out on the Mexico run-away with Josh. It was teasing, but it stung. Again, Andy the wimp.

SATURDAY, MARCH 3

Saturday was what most kids would consider a dream day. Although Andy had been grounded for misbehavior, his father took him hang gliding as a belated 15th birthday present. When he got home, his dad lifted his punishment to allow him to get together with his buddies.

Saturday night, Andy and a group of friends ended up partying in Josh's house. As the evening drew late, Williams says, he, A.J. and Josh all became drunk. He says Josh was angry at something Chris Reynolds had done to him and resurrected the shooting talk.

"My buddy, Josh, he went and got a sheet of paper and diagrammed the school. He said what hallway he was going to. He told A.J. where he was going to go. He told me where I was going to go."

Josh instructed Andy that he would be stationed in the boy's bathroom.

Williams says that Josh wanted him to use the .22 revolver in his dad's gun case, while Josh and A.J. Gilbert would take two small-gauge shotguns from the case and saw the barrels off for ease of concealment.

You say others learned about this? he was asked.

"Yeah, a bunch of people knew. Saturday night, we were telling everybody. Josh was telling everybody because he thought it was cool. I was telling everybody, hoping in the back of my mind that an adult would find out about it (and stop it). But every single person who was told about it seemed like they were encouraging it. Probably about 50 people total, including a couple of adults, knew about it. I think a lot of them didn't take it seriously."

What happened to the drawing?

"Josh threw it in the trash."

So, that indicated Josh was backing out of the scheme?

"Yeah."

SUNDAY, MARCH 4

Ironically, on Sunday afternoon, Andy's father took him to Lakeside to look at a condo they were planning to buy and relocate to, and which Andy liked. If he had so chosen, that move would have given him an escape—new school, new friends, fresh start.

"When we first talked about (the move), I said, 'Awesome.' I was getting away from these people. To me, it was like a positive thing. But, later, in my mind, I thought I was better off dying."

Sunday evening, Andy joined A.J. and Josh at a girl's house, and by that time he says Josh has changed the story and said that Andy was the one who Saturday night had bragged about shooting-up the school, and Andy went along with that version.

With the fresh memory of the Mexico-trip ridicule still burning in his ears, Andy did not back out. He says the infamous Columbine shooting of two years earlier never entered his mind as a template.

Apparently, his resolve wavered, and when he returned home Sunday night, he says he got a phone call from Chris Reynolds, who said to Andy that Josh had told him of the school-shooting scheme.

Williams says that Reynolds told him, "Listen, man, Josh told me everything, and if you don't go through with it, I'll kill you (myself)." Williams says he took that threat seriously because of the intimidating, mesmerizing presence of Reynolds in the lives of the boys.

MONDAY, MARCH 5

Sunday night, Andy didn't sleep well. He says he kept thinking about suicide. His last thought of the night was, "This is it." When he awoke Monday morning, it wasn't just another school day.

He says that neither on Sunday night nor Monday morning did he take drugs or drink alcohol.

"I got up and accepted that today I'm going to die. I'm glad it's over. I showered. I looked in the mirror. I got the key and opened the gun cabinet. I got out the pistol. I got the .22 bullets and put them on the bed." He found about 40 bullets, and took them all. (His father said later there was also a pellet pistol in the cabinet.)

Why, among the three of you, were you the one willing to go ahead?

"My whole plan was, I'm going to do this, and then I'm going to die. And so, I was just thinking about suicide the last couple of weeks, and I guess that was the day. If they (Josh and A.J.) didn't want to go through with it, I'm still going to die today."

Were you thinking of suicide by cop?

"Yes."

Rather than by your own hand?

"Yes. I mean, I had the gun in my mouth, and I was trying to figure out a way to do it so it wouldn't hurt. But after about eight months of pain, I didn't want my last experience on earth to be painful, you know what I mean?"

If you were shot by cops wouldn't that be painful?

"But I wouldn't know it was coming."

Early Monday morning, Williams says A.J. knocked on the door to return a bicycle that Andy had left at his house. "I told him he could have it because I didn't have any use for it anymore. A.J. said, 'I'm not gonna go through this with you.' He went into my room and he seen the pistol and the bullets on the bed, and he said, 'So you're still going to do it?' And I said, 'This is it for me.' And he said, 'All right.'

"I put the pistol and all the bullets in my backpack and went out to the bus stop. I was watching the cars go by, and thinking: whatever.

"We met up with the kids we usually met up with. A.J. was saying, 'All right, dude, nice knowing you.' And we kind of said our goodbyes again. He asked where I was going. I said the boy's bathroom, and he was, like, 'Man, you know most murders happen on a Monday.' I told him nobody was going to die."

Williams says he believed .22 bullets were not powerful enough to kill people. He says he had seen them bounce off coffee cans during target practice. He had bypassed the pellet pistol.

Shortly after 9 a.m., Williams says he took his backpack into a bathroom stall and closed the door. He nervously loaded the pistol and opened the door and saw standing beyond the stalls, at the urinals, freshman Bryan Zuckor, 14, and the taller Trevor Edwards, 17, a junior, who was directly in front. He decided he didn't want to shoot anyone he knew, so he closed the door. "I felt like, 'Dude, you either got to go through it or not, but you got to make a decision.' And I was, 'All right, I'm going to do it.'"

What was in your mind, standing in the bathroom stall?

"Like, I'm not somebody that's going to hurt people, and I was aware that what I was going to do was going to hurt somebody. But at the same time, I couldn't go back out to my friends—I can't go back out and put myself in a position that they're going to ridicule me. It was just the easiest way out."

He opened the stall door again and both boys were still there. "So I shut the door again, and I thought, 'Dude, what are you doing?' And I thought, I don't have it in me to hurt nobody. And then, for whatever reason, I was like, 'I'm going to open this door again, and if they're not there I'll pull the trigger. But if it is them, then I'm just going to walk out.' But when I opened up, I didn't see a tall dude in front of me so I pulled the trigger.

"I didn't know it was Bryan. I expected to see a tall person in front of me and a shorter dude to my right, but when I opened up the shorter guy was in front of me and the taller guy to the right."

You put the gun real close to the back of his head before you killed Bryan.

"I was about two feet away."

What went through your mind at that moment?

"Nothing."

Williams continues. "I (then) swung around and I shot Trevor. I think it hit him in the neck. He fell, and after about 10 to15 seconds he asked me why I did it. I told him to shut up.

Did you say that angrily?

"No, I was just—that was the only thing I could think of. That was a typical 15-year-old response to everything."

Williams says he knew Bryan from English class and liked him a lot. Trevor, he was less fond of, but had no deep animosity toward him. He then wounded student teacher Tim Estes as the few others in the bathroom scattered. As school security officer Peter Ruiz came in to investigate, he was wounded three times.

And then what?

"I reloaded and I guess I went out a little way and shot at people in the crowd, then I reloaded again."

Andy had gone to the doorway of the boy's bathroom and started shooting randomly at people walking in the area.

In all, Williams believes he reloaded four times and expended almost all of his 40 rounds. He wounded 13 persons, staff and students, and killed another boy, senior Randy Gordon, 17, whom he did not know.

When the police came, Andy hastily threw down the revolver and surrendered, as they demanded.

He was taken to the sheriff's office and interrogated. He gave as his reason that he was mad at how things were going (in his life). He told deputies, "I was just, like, screwing up in school and…I didn't want to move again, and my dad kept yelling at me. He's been bitching at me for a while. And everybody else is being stupid."

He also told deputies that he had not been bullied or even teased, and that neither parent had ever abused him.

Twelve years later, Williams says that—out of a young boy's misplaced bravado—he was ashamed to admit he had been bullied.

Asked if he intended to kill people, he told interrogators right after the shooting, "I didn't want anybody to die, but if they died, then, oh well."

Not long after the shooting, a forensic psychiatrist diagnosed him with a "major depressive disorder."

Andy spent a year and a half in juvenile hall where he was praised as a model inmate and did well in his schoolwork. He was in a controlled, protected environment—perhaps reminiscent of Twentynine Palms.

In August 2002 he instructed his public defender to plead him guilty to two counts of first-degree murder. He said he wanted to spare the wounded survivors and the families of the two murdered boys the pain of sitting through a trial.

He was sentenced to 50 years to life. He will be eligible for parole in his mid-60s.

Williams seems to have adjusted well to prison. The guards told me he is not considered a problem and are noticeably at ease with him. He's close to becoming a journeyman brick mason and is two classes short of an A.A. degree. He hopes to finish a bachelor's degree by correspondence.

He is kept in protective custody because he refused to stab another inmate at another prison, he says, a demand made on him by a prison gang. Because of that, for his own safety, he will never be allowed to leave protective custody, which suits him just fine.

He has a girlfriend who has been committed to him for several years. He has even thought of marriage, though lifers are not allowed conjugal visits. His father visits him monthly, and his mother flies in from Georgia at least twice a year.

He is quick to admit he deserved to be punished, and severely. He thinks the 50-year-minimum sentence was too much, considering his youth, but 20 years would have been too lenient. He believes 30 years would have at least given him the hope of someday having a positive life in society.

* * *

Have you ever thought of writing your victims?

"I'd like to, not necessarily to explain myself, but to pray that everything is going well with them, and to (let them) know how sorry I am. So whenever they're willing and ready to contact me, I'd love to (hear from them).

"I feel I owe it to them (the victims) not to mess up in here. I've already made a very bad decision that affected them, and I can't continue to make bad decisions. I want to be as productive and positive in here as I can."

Do you know who all 13 of your wounded victims are?

"I don't have them memorized, not anymore."

I ask if he's happy, and he says, "Reasonably. I have no complaints." But of life in prison, he says: "It's, like, it sucks. I hate it. But whatever you make of it, that's basically what it is. It can be miserable, if you let it. It's degrees of badness."

Does what you did ever hit you really hard, to this day?

"All the time. Like, what the hell did I do?"

Do you think of yourself as a murderer?

"I think it's hard to separate who I am from what I've done. Obviously, I committed that crime, so you'd have to classify me like that, but I don't necessarily think I intended to kill somebody, so therefore, like, I'm a killer. I do know that the people I shot did not deserve to be killed or wounded, and I will never stop regretting that."

Do you dread March 5th coming around?

"Not anymore."

Did you for a while?"

"Absolutely. I wouldn't eat. I'd seclude myself from everybody. But after a while, that became just like a shell, you know what I mean? I don't necessarily treat it like it's every other day, but…

*   *   *

We can analyze Williams' account of March 5, 2001 and say that much of it makes no sense. He says it doesn't to him, either. There are incongruities in his story apparent to you and to me, so, what is the value of reading the words of Andy Williams?

That's an individual judgment. When talking about such crimes, the experts say much, but often know little. Angry people can say, "Give 'em the needle." But that's an ice cream emotion: it savors well at the moment, but soon melts. Sympathetic people can say that we should try to understand the abuse they suffered. To a point, yes, but not to the extent that it makes us diminish the damage done to innocent people.

Another thing we can all do is listen, and despair of our ignorance.

The grownup Andy Williams is a pleasant guy with no evident antagonisms. But he's in prison. Most cons are the same way— while they're in prison. Anyway, that doesn't tell us why the child that he was went off the tracks.

One of his evident problems was that he wasn't aggressive and wouldn't fight. But why should someone have to fight not to be bullied, if indeed, bullied he was?

He says he was bullied at school, but the school denies it. But, really, how good are schools at detecting (and disclosing) the extent of bullying?

Andy chose his friends and became as one with them. They were troubled kids, all. His three main "homeboys" became horsemen of their own apocalypse.

Abri Joe "A.J." Gilbert, 23, died in 2008 while on parole after serving a year on a drug offense; Shaun Thomas Turk, 27, is serving time for murder, in the same prison as Williams; Joshua D. Stevens, 27, is in prison in Florida on a probation violation.

This is an old, familiar theme, but Andy was a latchkey kid— coming home from school to an empty house and free to roam. Free to get into whatever mischief appealed at the moment.

Andy had loving parents, though separate, and by planning to move to Lakeside, his father offered the golden opportunity to start fresh. But Andy turned away from it.

His father was not a disciplinarian, but isn't permissiveness our parenting philosophy du jour?

Williams turned his youth into a crime story, and helping other children avoid doing the same is our job. All of ours. And we can do that without excusing Andy Williams.

An internet site lists 115 school shootings in the U.S. since 1980, and the pace has been accelerating. Many of the other school shooters are dead. Andy Williams is alive and available to listen to.

It's only my guess, but I suspect he thought a guy with a gun comes across as really tough, with the added benefit that no one punches the dude with a gun. And no one ridicules him, either. This was a way to show everyone the real Andy Williams. He could make his own movie.

However, speculation aside, to understand the mind of any person is to walk down a hallway with many closed doors, not knowing behind which is concealed the truth we seek.

Andy Williams did not torture small animals, set fires to watch them burn, or bully smaller children—the usual mass-shooting indicators. And, had March 5 not happened, and were he on the street today, I strongly suspect he'd be a law-abiding working guy with a family.

At this point, what we are left with is to repeat a question that Williams asks, "What the hell did I do?"

That's right, Andy. What the hell did you do?

San Diego Union-Tribune, May 12, 2013

My life with the knife

The surgeon, like any other professional, functions mainly by routine—except for the patients, they're never routine.

No one knows that better than retired surgeon Ira Levine, 72, of San Diego

Levine says, "I had one 32-year-old patient, a striking woman from Ethiopia, a positive person with happy eyes and beautiful dark skin. She badly wanted children, but had suffered three miscarriages. She is a medical technician who came in with two breast cancers. After pre-operative chemotherapy, I removed the breast partially and also the lymph nodes. We discharged her with no evidence of cancer."

Howard Lipin, Union-Tribune

Ira Levine, M.D.

However, bad news returned eight months later when the radiation oncologist discovered a tumor in her armpit. She also had tests that indicated it was the most aggressive of tumors.

"A month later, we did a complete mastectomy with reconstruction and removal of more armpit lymph nodes. At that point, her survival prognosis was approximately 80 percent over five years."

(Levine is not comfortable putting people's lives in percentiles, but, in medicine, that is sort of the balance sheet.)

"I talked to her the other day, seven years later, and she is still a buoyant person, cancer-free and pregnant with her second child.

Many times, cancer treatment gives us renewed hope for happy lives, just like hers. It's quite amazing."

But not always, and in ways sometimes crushing to the spirit.

A patient was referred to Levine for possible surgery about six years ago. She was a college professor in her 30s with advanced breast cancer. Because of the size of the tumor, Levine recommended chemo prior to surgery.

"Astonishingly, she refused. She said she had suffered enough from other medical issues and didn't want any more. Her boyfriend had left her, and her spirits were obviously down. But she said something else that was shocking—she said her family had told her she deserved to have cancer.

"I don't know why she said that, or why her family said that, and I didn't pry. You learn soon enough that you can't help people who don't want to be helped.

"She never came back to see me. I lost track of her until I read her obituary."

* * *

The word "surgeon" is heavy footsteps in our ear because some stranger who holds that job will likely someday put us on a table and stick a knife into us; it'll be for our own good, but still, it's a knife. The surgeon is like a cop—we're intrigued to meet them, but prefer it under social circumstances.

He is asked about post-surgery malaise where the patient's energy level does not rebound until long after the bandages are removed. Is it reality or myth?

"It exists, absolutely. I think physicians need to be honest with their patients as to what's going to happen after surgery. There is no question it takes much longer to get over it than we might tell them. And as one ages, it takes even longer."

Is the malaise physiological or psychological?

Both. It's primarily physiologic, but if you can't do what you want to do, then it's gets between your ears. The only treatment is patience, family encouragement, and just do small tasks."

Over the years, you've obviously lost people.

"Very rarely. Lay people think medicine is a life-and-death business, but it's seldom that way, even for a general surgeon."

He says that of his approximately 10,000 operations, far less than 1 percent died as a result of complications, and many of those were expected, given their condition. Most times it happened in intensive care, not on the operating table.

What are your thoughts when you lose a patient?

"It's the worst feeling in the world. It's a terrible, depressing feeling, especially when you know the surgery went well. You question the decisions you made, you question your ability. You think, am I really up to this? But the self-doubt passes, and you go back to work."

And then, after that sad event, the family awaits...

"You've got to go out and talk to them."

Do they sometimes get angry at you?

"Yes, but you just do the best you can."

As do most physicians, Levine had a sense that mortality was all around him. He even had a personal yardstick for patient survivability which he tied to failings of body systems; for example, renal failure, pulmonary failure or poor cardiac function. "I developed a rule that if you are over 90, you can't have more than one complication. If you are over 80, more than two; over 70, more than three; or over 60, more than four. And if you did, your chance of surviving was greatly lessened."

He remembers a 93-year-old female patient in intensive care who was on dialysis with renal failure, respiratory failure and had a failing heart.

"One day I walked into the ICU, and she was being visited by one of her relatives. I said, 'It really isn't nice to keep this woman going on dialysis, on these cardiac medicines or the ventilator. If we stopped any one of them she would die.' And I said, 'In fact, we treat our dogs better than we are treating this woman, because we put them down when they are not well, and we know when to do that.'"

Were you urging the person to say, end it?

"I was indirectly urging that.

"So I went home and was immediately called. I was told that her granddaughter was very upset. She was put on the phone, and said, 'What do you mean, I'm treating my grandmother like a dog?' And I said, 'I didn't say that. I said you are treating your grandmother worse than a dog, because we know how to kindly put our pets down when they are not doing well. And if we were to stop this medicine right now, your grandmother would die. If we were to turn the ventilator off, your grandmother would die. If we were to stop the kidney machine, she would die. So there is nothing that we are doing that's keeping her alive except artificially. And I think she wouldn't want that. It's cruel and inhuman punishment.'

"(Consequently,) the granddaughter told the nurses to stop the treatment. The woman was dead in four hours."

* * *

The worst kept secret in medicine is that most doctors, at one time or another, assist in easing a patient into death.

"A long-time patient of mine had far advanced colon cancer and came in with metastasis, both in the liver and lungs. He was dying. He looked at me, and said, 'Please, just make me comfortable.' He made it clear he wanted to die. I explained what I proposed doing, and he agreed.

"So I wrote orders to give him increasing doses of morphine; enough morphine to make him go to sleep and die. It's really euthanasia, but it's disguised as making them comfortable. And after I wrote the orders, I went to his nurse and said, 'You know what we're doing here?' She said, 'Yes, I do.' I said, 'Are you comfortable doing it?' She said, 'Yes, I am.' The man died within 12 hours."

Levine is unafraid to question his own judgment. He recalls an operation that went well, but had an eventual bad ending. He did an emergency operation on a woman in her 80s with a hole in her large intestine. Feces was escaping into the abdominal cavity and she was in shock. The operation was successful and she was given a colostomy bag.

Later, she asked for the bag to be reversed and removed. Levine had his doubts, but performed the operation. The woman had a post-surgery stroke and died. In retrospect, he believes he should have refused to do the second surgery.

Levine learned an important and humane lesson when a friend was lying comatose with a severe stroke. Though the man couldn't respond, Levine would often go to his bedside and chat about the Padres, the weather, or whatever came to mind.

The man made an unexpected recovery, and Levine asked if he had heard what had been said to him.

"He looked at me, and said, 'Ira, I heard every word.' That gave me the shivers. From that moment on, I would tell families when patients were comatose, 'Talk to them, because my friend heard me.'"

* * *

Levine says before the knife cuts, there is always time to back off, and sometimes surgeons should.

"Once, early in my career, I asked a senior surgeon to assist me operate on a patient who had a complicated procedure to be done. On the morning of surgery, I went to see the patient, a woman in her 80s. I said, 'Are you ready for surgery?' She said, 'Doctor, to tell you the truth, I don't feel good about this operation.' And I said, 'If you don't feel comfortable about it, we won't do it and I'll cancel it.'"

Regardless of the reason?

"Regardless of the reason. I called the surgeon that was going to help me, and he was irritated. He had set aside the time, and he said, 'You got to talk her into it.' I said, 'She doesn't feel good about it, and I'm not going to do it.' She died before the next morning.

"One of the things I learned is—listen to the patient."

Do you remember your very first operation?

"No, but I'm sure I was scared. The scalpel is razor sharp. You'd be surprised how sharp it really is. It's very difficult to know what amount of pressure to put on your hand to cut through skin.

"I was doing a mastectomy about a dozen years ago, and an intern was helping me. I gave him a scalpel to make a small incision to put in a drain. He sliced almost as lightly as you would with a fingernail, just made a little redness. I told him he had to push just a little harder to get through the skin. But then he pushed too hard and cut through the muscles in the chest and into the lung. So instead of asking for a drain, I said, 'Can I have a chest tube?'

"One of the things we say in surgery is experience comes from bad judgment, and good judgment comes from experience."

Levine's attitude toward surgery is, "What's the hurry? There's always enough time to do it right. Some surgeons think they are really terrific if they can do it quick, and boast, 'I did it skin-to-skin in 30 minutes.' And then they have complications."

How about surgeries that are done for the surgeon's income?

"I'd like to think that doesn't happen, but I don't want to be naïve because clearly there are doctors that have done that, and some have gotten away with it, and many haven't.

"My cardinal rule was to care for patients as I would want to be cared for, and to treat them like a preposition—do something *for* the patient, not *to* the patient."

What specific operation would cause you to wake up in the morning and say, 'Oh, I have to do *that* today!'?

"None."

How tough is it to operate on severely obese people?

"Very difficult, very tough, because their abdominal wall is very thick from fat, and it increases the chances of infection."

Levine does not shy away from what he sees as the overuse or even misuse of endoscopic and robotic surgery.

Endoscopic surgery is done by inserting fiberoptics through small holes and manipulating instruments at the patient's side. Robotic surgery is operating by using instruments remotely with a monitor and sitting some distance from the patient.

Levine says both methods are useful, but what's happening today are more and more surgeons are using them for operations that don't need to be done that way, ignoring that conventional surgery would give the same results and possibly be better for the patient.

"Robotic surgery sounds sexier to the patient, but it's expensive, and not always desirable or even sensible."

As an example, he says surgeons are learning to take out the thyroid gland endoscopically. "I did a great many of those operations, and I don't see a need for it. I think you can be much safer looking with loupes (glasses worn to magnify tissues).

"Just recently, I talked to a colleague who said a number of general surgeons are also using robotics to take out gallbladders. And I asked, 'Why are they doing that? It's just an unnecessary increase in cost.'"

I asked an OB/GYN who had just finished a simple hysterectomy, not a complicated operation. The doctor told me it was done robotically, and I asked why. The reply was, 'Because it's fun.' And I said, 'Fun? It's overkill.'"

What are your impressions of our general health?

"Organic food, I think, will be shown to be little or no healthier than non-organic food. I also believe many products and over-the-counter medicines that promise to allow you to live longer, sleep better, etcetera, will be proven to be valueless.

"There are five things that Americans can do that will reduce health risks dramatically: eat in moderation, drink in moderation, exercise, don't smoke, and wear seatbelts. And you don't need a doctor to tell you any of those things."

Today, Levine can sit in their home above San Diego where he and wife, Ellen, raised three children and reflect on those decades in medicine. In hindsight, he doesn't see disease, he sees healing. He doesn't see pain, he sees relief. And his golf game is coming around.

San Diego Union-Tribune, May 26, 2014

Convicted killer's wife struggles with tragedy

Tamara Vilkin

The Vista, Calif. courtroom is locked in that kind of quiet when even the breathing is shallow. Everyone looks straight ahead. On one side of the room are the victim's family and friends; on the other are a smaller number for the defendant. All are waiting.

Finally, maddeningly slow, lawyers and the defendant stand as jurors file in and take their seats, verdict in hand. It's June 20: the day of reckoning for Michael Vilkin.

Vilkin, 62, is a Russian émigré of some 30 years ago; a small man of gray beard who has never been in trouble. He was an economist in his home country, but has been unable to find meaningful work in California. He is said to be mild-mannered and kind.

Others say he's a murderer. That on March 28, 2013, because of a two-year property dispute on Lone Jack Road in Encinitas, he took a large handgun and shot neighbor John Upton to death.

The people of the State of California called it murder in the first degree.

In the tense courtroom, the verdict is read, and the jury agrees: guilty.

Unless an appellate court should rule otherwise, Michael Vilkin's life as a free man is over.

(No matter what the dispute between the two men, by every account, John Upton was a philanthropic man with a generous spirit.)

No one in the courtroom is greatly surprised. Except one.

A stunned woman in the second row believed the jury would acquit Vilkin. And she will always insist he acted in self-defense. If the whole world believes Vilkin is guilty, then the whole world is wrong.

She is a quiet woman holding an open Bible. Her clothes drape because she has lost 20 pounds. The grief diet. She seems fragile, and has made no attempt to emotionally protect herself from the thunder clap of the law that she thought would not happen.

Day after day of the trial she sat in the same seat reading her Bible, especially the book of Job, searching for strength and answers to the anguish that descended on her like a plague of locusts.

Next to her, ever faithful, were women from her church and parents of her piano students giving support to a woman they love.

* * *

The jury did what the jury did. My interest is that woman.

If you imagine a small woman of 56 with a hint of gray in her auburn hair, with granny glasses and a patient, soft voice, proper but not quite prim, whose anger would top off at a frown, then you would have the image of the grandma everyone would like to have had. And, yes, you would also have Tamara Vilkin, a gentle piano teacher who would hug a whinny, tone-deaf adolescent.

Tamara was born in Minsk, Belarus. Back then, it was part of the Soviet Union. Her father ran off when she was 8 months old.

"It was me and my mom and it was not an easy life. Sometimes it was not enough money to get from one salary to another, but we survived. She was working in construction. It was a cold place to work on the road.

"In spite of all of this, she was willing to pay for my piano lessons. I tried my best and I graduated from music college."

In 1982 she met her husband, Michael, an economist. Soon after marriage, they decided to emigrate from mother Russia. However, at that time, the Soviet Union had stopped issuing visas, but by his signaling that he wanted to leave, Michael was labeled a "refusenik," and became tainted for any good jobs. He ended up stocking store shelves, but continued to petition to leave the country.

Exit visas were finally granted 5 years later, and the couple first went to Vienna, and eventually made their way to New York City in 1987.

Other than jobs such as security guard, Michael had a tough time finding a place in our economy. A Soviet-trained economist was not a smooth fit in a capitalist system. Tamara the piano teacher was the main support for many years.

"We had not much money, but life is not about money always. My husband is very optimistic man. He's the fun man. He's loving man. We were very close," Tamara says.

Michael earned an MBA degree and continued to write about the economy, but paying jobs remained elusive.

"In 2008 we bought the land in Encinitas. Then the trouble started," she says.

The 2.6-acre unimproved parcel on Lone Jack Road was going to be their retirement nest egg. But, a conflict over ownership of an access road developed with the neighboring landowner. Eventually, somehow, Upton,

a renter, became involved.

"Michael worked very hard over there. It was a jungle when we bought it. It's a lot of dead brush and dead trees. He just himself, he cleaned so much over there. He did beautiful job. We were waiting and waiting; maybe the bank will start lending money. Maybe we will build a house, but it never happened because of the problems."

Tamara says she knew Michael had bought a gun, but he tended to keep troubles internal, so she never learned just how toxic the situation on Lone Jack Road had become.

On the day of the shooting, she tried to call his cell phone several times without success. Finally, she drove over. There, she saw flashing lights, and police and media all over. She asked someone what had happened, and she was told someone had been killed. She immediately assumed it was Michael.

What exactly did happen? Stuff happened, and that's a polite noun. There's no point in rehashing what a jury has ruled.

* * *

A month has passed, and Tamara's tears have dried into sad resolve. She has been warned that appellate courts are hard to convince, but she will push ahead with an appeal, though it could exhaust her remaining assets.

"One of the correspondent called me, a young girl. She said, 'Mrs. Vilkin, I understand what you're going through.' I told her, 'How old are you?' She said, 'I'm 27.' I said, 'Darling, you have no idea what you're talking about. You don't understand what I'm going through.'

"When very beginning when Michael was arrested and he was in jail, I live on the second floor and every time somebody walks on the stairs, I was thinking it was him.

"That's how mind is just playing games with me sometimes. There's nothing changed for me. My husband is my life and I decided even if he is going to spend the rest of his life in prison, we are going to build our life just around this. If he will be in prison, I will visit him. We will talk. We will write. There's nothing can break connection I have with this man. This is impossible to break."

She expresses condolence to the Upton family for having lost a loved one, but you can tell she firmly believes John Upton caused the confrontation that resulted in his death. She will never be persuaded otherwise.

Tamara has a visceral need to proclaim Michael's innocence, that he was provoked, threatened and feared for his life; that he believed a cell phone John Upton was carrying was a gun and his life was in danger. Michael, she is absolutely certain, was too decent and kind to commit such a heinous crime without fear and provocation.

"I don't care what people think, because I know who Michael is, and I know his soul is clean."

She wants the world to know all this, and to believe as she does. But the media is moving on, the lawyers have other cases, the jurors have returned to their jobs, and soon there will be no one to listen.

The love of a woman for a man is a thing both glorious and terrifying. It can make the heart beautiful, but can also put the burden of heavy stones on the spirit.

John Upton's family and friends would say the same things that Tamara is saying, that he was too decent and kind a man to die in a dusty field.

A good man is dead, and another's life is in ruins.

There is something primeval about all this. What is it about a house or a plot of land that can turn neighbors into enemies? Every cop on patrol has stories of arguments mediated and fights stopped because of some boundary dispute, an untrimmed tree or a barking dog. And, yes, it can turn deadly.

The worst has happened, and Tamara's life will never again be the same. Her soul bleeds from a wound she will never allow to heal. She is Michael's wife. She loved him for better, now she will love him for worse.

"Horrible thing has happened in my life and I cannot fix it. I live in this nightmare for a long time."

If you have no charity for this faithful wife, then your heart is too hard.

San Diego Union-Tribune, July 21, 2014

Animals come to the rescue of striving girl

Giovanna Camunez

Notsu and Happy will soon join Mufasa in becoming steaks, but their sacrifice will be for a good cause.

Because these three steers will have taken their place on the dinner table, a young woman will have found a fuller meaning for her life.

Well, there is more to it than that, but for Giovanna Camunez of Oceanside, Calif., taking on these animals for a high school FFA (Future Farmers of America) project could be the turn-around point of a young life going nowhere and pointed in a wrong direction.

My partner-wife, Kathy, was walking among the cattle pens at the county fair. She stopped and beckoned me to meet a young woman fussing with two animals and happy to be doing it. Giovanna was short, vigorous, open-faced and chatty with a stranger. However, something about her was different from the typical Valley Center farm kid.

She has spent almost all her 18 years in an east Oceanside housing pocket north of route 76. It's a place where 'hood "role models" pied-piper kids down a twisting path that will more likely lead to jail than college. Or down the road to nearby Eternal Hills. A reminder of that final destination is a "monument" just down the street from Giovanna's family home to a dead youth who ran afoul of his peers.

Giovanna gives a macabre verbal tour: "What happened was a murder right down the street. It's actually a couple houses down. That was my brother's best friend. It was a drive-by and they killed him. There's a cross there."

And then, in a park, a block or two away: "There was a kill of a teenage couple right in the park. That's why there's lights there now." She also recalls two other young people murdered in that park a few years ago.

The first neighborhood "elementary" lesson is survival. It's a primer studied on the street, and often in the home. You learn quickly to "get along by going along," which is the same lesson taught in La Jolla except the destinations are different. Violence is not only a tool, it's also a business plan, administered by gangs capable of nine-millimeter discipline.

"Yeah, there's a lot of gangs," Giovanna says. "I'm scared. They know me by my brothers, because my brothers are well respected. I'm perfectly safe, but at the same time, I don't feel comfortable."

We sit at a small table in the small house that Giovanna recently called home. The house has two bedrooms, plus an add-on room, plus a garage bedroom. The living set-up is dormitory. Giovanna says she lived four years in this house with lots of people, three dogs, three cats, crowded bedrooms, and two bathrooms.

How many people live here?

She pauses. "I have no idea. I haven't counted." But then, she ticks off on her fingers: "Right now I think it's one, two, three, four, five, six, seven…I think eight to 10 people."

That live in this house?

"No, nine. Nine people, yeah, right now."

She now lives not far away in a two-bedroom apartment with her boy- friend, along with a woman with a son. Asked why she moved out, she says, "It's kinda cramped here."

She grew up with a brother, a half-brother and three half-sisters. Her widowed mother, Raquel, still lives there. She is a friendly woman who speaks only "get-by" English. Her father is dead, but that requires more than four words in this story.

Giovanna's early life promised nothing for her future. Her two brothers had gang involvement and brushes with the law in the past; two sisters got pregnant early and the third left home at 18.

Giovanna was a tough kid. She wanted to construct a don't-mess-with-me aura which would protect her and also gain approval from her brothers.

"No one messed with me. I was actually trying to be like my brothers, trying to be those big guys. I was a girl, yeah, but it doesn't mean you can mess with me."

You would fight other girls?

"Yeah. I got in trouble a lot for getting in fights."

Why?

Because I looked up to my brothers. I saw how they were so respected in the neighborhood. I wanted to be like that. I wanted to be well respected. In my sophomore year, I was actually kind of getting my act together. I was actually studying, but at the same time, when someone made a comment during class, I got up, I walked over to them and I told them to shut up or we can take it up outside.

"I had the muscle and the build to back it up. I still do. I've gotten a little chubby, but I've still got it."

But you're not a fighter anymore.

Huge smile. "I'm a lover now."

For her actions, Giovanna barely avoided continuation school, which is generally for troubled kids. However, she was assigned to independent study for her final two years. That meant she did her work outside class and met with instructors once a week.

She could handle all that, but it was the death of her 50-year-old father, Adolfo, that continued to grip her spirit and wouldn't let her escape.

Adolfo was a self-employed tow-truck driver and Giovanna's hero. She still calls herself a "daddy's girl." Her fondest memory is riding along on calls with him at 2 a.m. and sitting high up in the truck cab to share his world.

"Dad tried giving his legacy to my two brothers, but they didn't want it. Me, I was into it. It made me happy to be bonding with my dad and him letting me be a part of it.

"Actually I was his princess, because two sisters, they got pregnant at a young age. The other sister ran away twice. My dad invested so much money to find her the first time she ran away; the second time he didn't even care. He was like, She's gonna come back anyway, sooner or later."

Four years ago, her father's murdered body was found alongside a road in Tijuana, wrapped in a blanket. His pick-up truck was found nearby, smashed. The crime was never solved.

"I was really depressed. I was cutting myself, trying to harm myself. I tried committing suicide. The week of the funeral, I found these pills my dad had and I took them. I took like six."

Do you know what they were?

"They were for his digestive system, so I had the runs for a good couple days."

Giovanna carries the burden of her father's death sadly but proudly. He was the one who made her feel special. It has left her with competing ambitions: She wants to be a veterinarian but also run a tow-truck company in her father's memory.

Implausible? That's okay. She's 18. Time will sort it out. But the towing ambition shows a good heart, and the veterinarian ambition shows a new-born awareness of a better world.

She has earned her high school diploma while supporting herself with a near-full-time job bagging groceries. And perhaps thinking of her sisters, she says she won't get married or pregnant until her 30s.

* * *

At the beginning of her junior year, Giovanna discovered her softer side—not for people, a species often not to be trusted in her purview—but for what the ancients called a "beast of the field."

She somehow came across an FFA project for students to adopt farm animals as projects. She talked her way into the program and was able to borrow money from a special fund. She bought a year-old steer, named him Mufasa, and promptly fell in love.

"I just grew very soft when I started raising Mufasa. Honestly, he saved my life from a lot of things. It just made me so happy just how sweet he was when I would get there. He'd moo because my old car had a huge muffler, so he'd actually hear it when I'd come in. I'd play with him. It hurt me so bad to let him go, but that's the reason I raised him for. I know that. But he changed me in soooo many ways."

She spent hours currying and feeding Mufasa, starting every day at 6 a.m. When she sold him at the 2014 fair, she broke even after feed costs and paying off her loan.

Last year, after having proved herself, she bought two calves and named them Happy and Notsu. They were also shorthorn-angus crosses. She calls them "cows," but as a term of affection. A new love affair was born.

"I wouldn't say they were smart. I think they were just smart in understanding me. Every time they were laying down, I would sit there and talk to them. I'd tell them how my day was and then ask how their day was. I do think they have feelings because Notsu would just put his face on me and I'd just rub him. His huge head would fall asleep on my lap. Same thing with Happy.

"They just changed me. I have no idea how. I felt so much more comfortable to be myself instead of being so tough and hard and having my guard up and everything."

This girl never was a tough kid. Inside, she was just a softie whose heart was scratching against the wall to be set free.

At the end of this year's fair, Giovanna sold her two beeves, and after subtracting her costs and debts, turned a profit of $3,000. She tries not to think of her animals' fate, but knows the slaughter house is always the eventual end. She also knows that farm animals will exit her life as she pursues other goals.

Looking back, she says, "It makes me cry. I know for a fact my dad's looking down on me and telling me he's proud of me. I graduated with A's and B's. I didn't get pregnant. I feel very proud of myself. I have never told myself that until I picked up my cap and gown."

She has glimpsed a vision of a better life, and this fall will enter Palomar College. Giovanna will continue her quest for all the exciting things she is destined to learn about this lively, interesting person that "cows" fall in love with.

* * *

A girl being turned around by an FFA project makes a great story, but the three steers were only a means, not a reason. The true impetus of her growth came from something wispy and hidden inside her that has made her look inward and upward, rather than outward and downward.

The challenge now for Giovanna is to keep her grip on the ladder. She is bright, assertive, and unafraid of the unknown. However, the grimness of her earlier years will not give up easily. As she moves into a more genteel but challenging area of society, every little slight, real or imagined, will cause her past to whisper, "You're not good enough. Come home."

She will have to answer that voice.

San Diego Union-Tribune, July 27, 2015

'I thought it was a big squirrel'

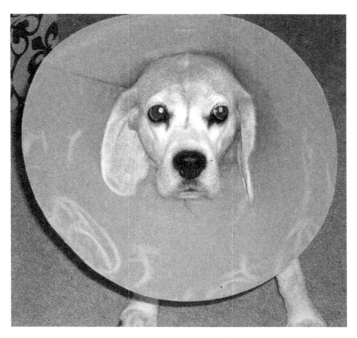

Moxie can't lick her wounds

"Y ou need to write something lighter," my wife, Kathy, lectured. "You've been writing too much sad stuff. Write about what happened to Moxie (our beagle)."

"You think that's not sad stuff?" I said. "Moxie was attacked. She was in agonizing pain. The poor little creature was brutalized."

"Well, you could write it humorously."

* * *

Where to start? It was an eventful day for us and our runty beagle. 'Eventful' usually means expensive.

Uneventful days for Moxie consist of sleeping 18 hours, eating two meals and begging for six more, and guarding the house from the deck against leashed terriers out on a walk, but with furtive behavior that makes Moxie watchful of a sudden move to take over her territory. You can't trust sneaky dogs.

* * *

But back to the (more interesting) other kind of day.

It became eventful the moment a raccoon waddled by, intent on finding an unguarded koi fish pond. It was only being a coon, which can be irritating to koi owners.

Suburbanite raccoons no longer seek meals in creeks for little one-bite fish; , which has a poor cost-benefit ratio. That is so yesterday. They now dine on plate scrapings of filet mignon in Del Mar garbage cans. Of course, nailing a fat carp in a backyard pond is a piece of cake (actually, a fish), even if a coon's skills are rusty.

An urban raccoon can range from 15 pounds up to gastric-bypass weight, depending on the security of garbage can lids. However, in a fight, no raccoon is small. Those 15 pounds include 10 pounds of claws. Though they look cute, which they are as a stuffed toy, don't be fooled. They're wolverines with an arthritic walk.

They say raccoons are prey to coyotes, but I'll tell you what— that's got to be one tough coyote willing to pay for its dinner.

When humans seek to prove their stupidity, coons are happy to oblige.

It's been known to happen in the rugged Sierra wilderness, between the Yosemite Lodge gift shop and the bus stop, that foreign tourists from Japan or New York rush for medical help holding a bloody hand out in front like a bowling trophy. The raccoon watches them run away while spitting out a finger. Doritos are preferred.

The ranger postings warn not to feed the animals. Apparently, the signs don't have room to mention no petting.

Down south, a "coon dog" hasn't earned the title if it doesn't have as many scars as a daydreaming butcher.

So, what skin does Moxie have in this game? Beagles aren't guardians of gentrified carp.

First, a word about the pampered Moxie. She's a cuddly pet to us "owners"—Can I still say that? Some pursed-lip souls oozing with unctuous, preening sentimentality take offense at the "owner" label. They prefer "guardian," or "companion." Even "pet parent" is suggested. However, that might be awkward for a woman who becomes "parent," to a male dog.

However, a cute dog is not universally loved. To rabbits and ground squirrels, Moxie's a terrorist deserving of a gallon of water-boarding.

She'd make her living hunting little rodents full time if she weren't already on welfare.

Moxie stares through a patio door by the hour at a hole in the fence where a ground squirrel briefly surfaced back in 2015. Eternal vigilance is the price of, well, killing a rodent. Surely, hers is a study in determination and patience, but on the other hand, she has nothing else to focus on except the aforementioned eating and sleeping. A vet's knife has taken sex off the table—no, strike "table." I recoil at the image.

I once had a boss who would doggedly stare like Moxie while monitoring the office coffee machine.

Yes, dogs snore, and they dream, too, which is apparent by restless yipping in mid-slumber. About what, I can't imagine (see "sex" above). Maybe she's the regal Buck in "Call of the Wild." However, Jack London would never have created an undersized beagle as a noble canine protagonist.

Someone once advised that a touch of mineral oil in Moxie's food would make her coat shiny. Well, yes, it does that, but I won't tell you what else it does, this being breakfast time.

* * *

Anyway, back to the showdown in suburbia. You know by now that dog and coon are going to meet, right? And revenge for the rodent nation will ensue, right? I foreshadowed that. Well, when they did, the fur flew, which is what we say when a better metaphor hides from us.

It started when Moxie was making one of her appointed rounds in the backyard. All of a sudden, she sees this—What? Giant ground squirrel? A Boone and Crockett record?...Well, big and fat, but manageable. This is what I do.

The battle lasted about 10 seconds, but must have seemed forever to one of the combatants. Guess which one?

Moxie ended the fight by doing what she could do and the coon couldn't—yelp and run like hell. And if a smirking rabbit were watching? Too much to bear.

There were two winners and two losers in this bout. The coon remains undefeated and waddled away with a great brag to take back to the den. The bloodied loser was Moxie. Joining her in doleful defeat were her human companions: Kathy, the treasured companion, and I, the tolerated one.

The other winner was the veterinarian (sponsor of the coon, I believe) who joined the raccoon in the winner's circle $904 richer, and cooing sympathetic condolences that not for one minute did I believe.

Moxie emerged from the vet's clinic stitched-up like a pet companion to Frankenstein's monster, wearing a cone on her head like an alien in a 1950s sci-fi movie. Maybe she should be allowed to lick her wounds. She sure as hell couldn't lick the coon.

My next dog is going to be a three-legged pug named Tripod that'll hobble away in panic from a backyard gopher.

San Diego Union-Tribune, June 13, 2016

Growing up with drugs in the home

Joey Lattarulo

"Like father like son" is a hoary old cliché so familiar that its warning usually earns a shrug, even though human behavior says it's true. Euripides, that wise old Greek, cautioned the same thing 2,500 years ago, as he wrote, "The gods visit the sins of the fathers upon the children."

Not a lot has changed in a couple of millennia. To make the unhappy point, a young hoodlum in juvenile hall will often mention (and proudly) a father who once looked through the same bars.

A childhood from hell can be overcome, but so can Mt. Everest.

Any child—boy or girl—is the captive of environment, and if it's a drug-infested home, then that becomes his classroom, and the family are his tutors. The life they live becomes his normal. Whatever the warnings, the child of a drug addict is still his father's son.

Even a youth who pulls his feet out of that quicksand must make his peace with ugly experiences no child should have, and that's what made Joey Lattarulo old and wise beyond his 18 years.

Joey is a senior at Oceanside (Calif.) High School. He's small and slight with curly black hair and a wisp of a beard. Unlike many peers, he engages with eye contact and speaks thoughtful words; no giggler he. Joey's an honor roll student who serves as aide to his English teacher.

He participates in music, swimming and water polo. Most of Joey's friends are girls and he prefers to socialize with them, including with his actual girlfriend. Unusual for his age, he's religious and prays a lot. He also works part-time in a restaurant to save for college.

* * *

Even more unusual, from infancy up to his junior year in high school, Joey lived in a home where crystal meth occupied the honored seat at the table. It was a tweaker way-station and the meth version of a crack house.

Joey was born into chaos. His mother left him and three older sisters when he was still an infant. "She went off and did her partying. Her justification was that she didn't want to drag us into the mud with her. (But) she could have chosen us over that. That's when the bad things started, (when) she left."

For the rest of Joey's childhood his mother was in and out of his life, mostly out.

The jumble of events placed Joey in a foster home at about age 6 which he recalls as a horrible time. When he was told one day that a family member would be picking him up soon, Joey sat on the front steps by the hour, day after day, until he saw his aunt drive up to deliver him from the nightmarish place.

He thinks that experience made him desperate to stay with his family, no matter how bad it became. Such as it was, it was home.

His father had been given custody at the time of the split, and the family lived in a two-bedroom apartment on Clementine Street in downtown Oceanside where Joey says his father failed to control the girls. "My father tried to raise us on his own, at least he tried to. But my sisters just overran him. They never listened to what he said. He just had no power over them."

Though she had been several years mainly out of his life, Joey's most painful memory of his mother happened in middle-school at a time when she was staying at a house down the street. He noticed a couple of strange men driving around using binoculars. Shortly thereafter, he saw his mother running down the street screaming. The men, he found out, were bounty hunters who had come to take her away.

When his carpenter-handyman father was at work or out of the house, Joey as a young child would have to tag along with his sisters to wild teen parties where he sat in the corner and witnessed behavior not included in his Dick and Jane school texts.

* * *

The family moved to a little-better neighborhood when he was 10 or 11, and that is where Joey became aware of his dad using crystal meth. The girls soon followed their dad into substance abuse: the oldest into alcohol, and the other two into pot and mainly crystal meth. He says at least one teenage sister eventually did the drug alongside their father. The home turned into a 24-hour drug house attracting a parade of tweakers, he says.

Joey experienced three police raids, the first when he was 10 or 11 and was hosting a friend on a sleep-over. "It was scary. They kicked down the door and raided the whole house. It was just because my father had all these drug dealers in and out."

Joey weathered the shock of seeing his father handcuffed and arrested. At other times, both his middle and younger sisters were also arrested.

The house traffic was crowded by his middle sister's friends who were from well-known Oceanside street gangs. "She was dating some guy from one of those places and he would come around and bring his friends. I would always be so worried for her because there's like six guys marching into the house and I know they're all doing drugs."

* * *

Joey says his oldest sister was the only one who ended up doing something positive with her life later on. The middle sister was the one he was closest to as a child, but she was the one who descended most deeply into drugs.

"Having to watch all this every day was just a terrible thing. When someone is high on meth, they don't sleep. They're up all night and they are really not rational. They spontaneously do things; they clean all the time but never get anything done. They clean for an hour on one corner of the room to make it perfect and then everything else is just a disaster. You look into their eyes and you just don't see the same person."

He once visited his dad's job site and realized the appeal of meth to laboring men. "I was amazed that they were, like, all tweakers. They would go into the bathrooms and get high because it gives them so much more energy. My father, he has a lot of injuries. Every day he had a lot of pain. I saw how he got so addicted."

* * *

Joey was thrust into the role of babysitter when he was not yet a teenager. He recalls times his middle sister would go off and leave her infant children in his care. "I'm crying at the door asking her not to leave, but she would just walk out the door and just leave me there with her kids."

Joey's efforts to wean his family off drugs made him perhaps the youngest drug counselor ever.

"From third grade on I knew my family were meth addicts. That was just my life. My middle sister was always difficult to talk to. She would just cry and run away and yell at me. My youngest sister would talk to me. She would get emotional and tell me she knows that she's not doing the right thing; she knows she's better than that. But she never stepped out of it. She just kept going.

"My father would never admit anything to me, so I used to play detective. I would search the house and find their meth pipes and drugs. I would break them and leave them on his desk."

However, even with that evidence, his father would still claim he didn't use drugs. Joey says that he eventually wrote letters to his family members pouring out his young heart and asking that they stop using drugs. He got no return mail.

Joey had a slight scrape with that life himself, experimenting with marijuana and alcohol as a freshman, but says he did a reality check and turned his back on the things that had destroyed his family.

Early in his junior year, he moved in with his aunt and her husband in Carlsbad, even though leaving meant separating himself from his two infant nephews, for whom he had almost been an adolescent parent. But for the first time he was exposed to the normal life of a high school student.

"They took me in with open arms and I (experienced) what it's like to have a structured family, to have rules and people that actually parent you. Growing up, *I* was the parent, trying to tell my father what's right and wrong and what he shouldn't do."

Joey was also encouraged by teachers who saw his potential and convinced him to see it, too. He has won a Simon Family Foundation scholarship that will give him a start in college where he wants to study psychology. He already has been accepted by San Francisco State.

"I really want to understand and help—not just me and my family, but other people, too. I want to understand why my sisters fell so hard to drug addiction and my (older) sister did not. I want to understand why I didn't fall into that life.

"Going to college is proof that I can amount to anything I desire, as well as set an example for all the people in my family."

Joey says he loves his entire family and always will. His biggest resentment is that his father has never admitted nor apologized for the helter-skelter life he forced on Joey.

"I've sat down and talked to my parents (separately). My mom, she admits her faults and apologizes for them. My father doesn't. He's in denial. He always has been. When he would get mad, he was just raging mad. I just, I've always wanted my father to admit that he was a bad parent."

* * *

I was unable to contact Joey's sisters, but I reached his father who lives in another county.

The father started off explaining that Joey's mother was not on the scene and was of little help in raising him, obviously trying to shift blame. When I asked if he would confirm his crystal meth use and that of two daughters, the question was followed by a long pause. A silent response of shock and embarrassment oozed through the phone.

Finally, "Well…" he said in a whispery voice, perhaps stalling to find a better answer. Pressed, he acknowledged he and his daughters used meth, "a little bit." Then, finally, an unqualified, "yeah," to the same question for himself, but "not all" of the daughters.

The apology Joey wants was not mentioned because that shouldn't come through me. That is for his son to hear. Face to face. But until that day comes, Joey will be just fine.

San Diego Union-Tribune, February 10, 2014

An ironworker forged in devotion

Natasha Steagall and Cliff Steagall

If you're facing retired ironworker Cliff Steagall and accuse him of being a warm, sensitive human being, he'll likely look over his shoulder to see whom you're talking to.

Cliff is a fellow whose words don't travel around curves or corners. And if yours aren't straight, he'll grow wary. He spent his career climbing places that would make a cat queasy. The guys he was a part of don't blink when doing their job, but would be called crazy by those who value a long life.

However, when you enter Cliff's pleasant Chula Vista house, nothing is out of place, no magazines on the floor next to an easy chair; no empty coffee cups on an end table. Someone fastidious is in charge here, certainly not a hard-hat guy. But, yeah, it is. Cliff is a widower. Every doily was put in place by him.

Cliff lost his wife, Gladys, 6 years ago. After 47 years of marriage and three children, she died of emphysema in her own bed. He has stayed single, because, "I didn't want to get married again, because you're married by the Bible, divorced by the law, but the book also says until death do you part. I still feel like I'm married to my wife, even though she's out there in the graveyard."

He's also the grandfather and conservator for Natasha Steagall, 27, who has severe cerebral palsy. Natasha was born with a back that was crooked. Her legs were bent up underneath her. Her right foot was in a U, Cliff says.

Until 18 months ago, Natasha lived with him, but no longer. We'll come back to why that is.

Cliff details at length the extensive surgeries and therapies for Natasha that he and his late wife pursued. Finally, he says, "We straightened her out the best we could to where she would look normal. She actually looks normal."

Natasha has been educated through special education, and continues going to school. She is fully observant and can communicate—except that her words are clear in her mind, but her tongue won't allow their escape. She speaks in muffled monosyllables; Cliff, though, has learned her language.

"They tried to teach her sign, but she doesn't have the dexterity in her fingers to do that, so she says basics like 'Ma, Pa, eat, sick, done.' 'Poo,' when she has to go to the bathroom.

The two understand each other. Cliff says, "She'll say, 'Pa.' I'll say, 'What?' She'll say, 'Uh,' and point to the TV. I'll say, 'You want to watch TV?' She'll say, 'Yeah.'

"When she's hungry and she wants a drink, she'll say, 'Dink.' Just little things like that. Some words you can understand, some you can't. She wants to go someplace, she says, 'Mmm, Pa. Mmm.' I say, 'What?' She'll go, 'Mmm, mmm, mmm.' Mainly, she wants to go down to the desert and get in a Jeep and ride out over the hills. The rougher it is, the better she likes it."

Cliff says, proudly: "If I stand her up there with a walker, she can make pancakes. I give her all the mixture. She knows how much to put and everything. She can scramble eggs. She can't fry eggs. She burns them and messes them up."

"Her favorite TV program is 'Two and a Half Men.' She used to like that a lot," Cliff says.

How do you know that?

"Because she laughs at all the jokes."

The world Natasha occupies is a bare landscape to me. I ask Cliff: It's eerie that a person with an alert mind can express all her thoughts only with grunts. Do you think she has adjusted to that? Does it just become your life, the way it is?

"I imagine it's her normal. She doesn't know anything else. See, you and I only know the normal normal." He gives me a dry smile, the way men with calluses on their hands do each other. "Of course, I don't know how normal you are."

I laugh. "It comes and goes."

"Anyway, he says, letting the joke die, you and I, we know we can go get us a drink of water, or we can go to the bathroom by ourselves, or we can get in a car and drive down and get a hamburger. She's never known that. She doesn't miss it. You miss what you know."

When Gladys died he became sole caretaker of Natasha for 5 years. And for a man just turned 70, that was a daunting challenge—"daunting"? No, damned scary. But he did it.

Finally, though, he had to face facts: Though he had a part-time caretaker for Natasha, Cliff realized it was not enough, and his age and iffy health could put her in jeopardy.

"I couldn't do a lot of things anymore. My back went out. I got steel rods and six screws in my back. Sometimes I bend over and I have a hard time getting back up again. Being able to put her in a bathtub and get her out, I couldn't do it anymore, so I had to get some help.

"I already had two heart attacks. If I had a fatal one, what would happen to her? She could be here alone for God knows how long."

The solution a year and a half ago was to place Natasha in Noah Home, a large assisted living residence in Spring Valley.

He says, "She's on Medi-Cal and Social Security. That's what's paying for her being there, plus donations from me, whenever I can afford it. I'm on Social Security and a small pension, too. I'm pretty hands-on, so I volunteer at Noah whenever they need me."

As always happens in these partings, even though there was no choice, Cliff felt the weight of guilt of seeing her go, especially when he went by Natasha's room at night and looked in to see an empty bed.

When you made that decision, did you have a sense of failure?

"Oh, yes. Oh, yeah. I prayed to the Lord for strength. I felt like I had a purpose in life when I had my granddaughter."

According to Cliff, though, Natasha immediately adjusted to her new surroundings like a ship slipping into a berth. She even has found a boyfriend named Ryan, a resident who has a similar medical condition.

Her happiness acted like a balm to caress the pain out of his loneliness.

Natasha returns to Cliff's house, the only home she had ever known, maybe once a month, and stays the night. It has helped Cliff regain his emotional footing from one of the toughest decisions of his life.

"I do have a lady friend that comes over, and we go out to a movie or something. Then, she goes home, and I'm alone again." He makes a panorama wave of the house. "As you see, you look at the house, I haven't changed anything. My granddaughter's all over the place. It's like she's still here, you know?"

Walking down the hall, I look in an open door to a bedroom that looks like a motel room awaiting a visitor. I ask if that's a guest room.

He looks fondly past the door. "No. It's my granddaughter's bedroom." He looks at me to underscore the point. "Exclusively hers. It started out with a baby crib when she was 18 months old."

You won't let anyone else sleep in it?

A head shake. "I won't let anyone else sleep in it."

He continues. Mentioning the bedroom seems to tie everything together. "When she comes to spend the night, and then goes home (to Noah), I take the sheets off, wash them, clean them and everything. Put it all away and have it ready for when she comes next time."

He smiles at memories that others would try to force from their minds. "Well, for 5 years I was alone with Natasha here: Her getting sick, and you're up all night long with her throwing up and running temperatures. Then, throwing up in a bed and pooping her pants.

"I had to bathe her. When she started her period, I had to take care of all that. I worked with her day after day after day to try to walk. She does walk a little bit.

"I did what I had to do, and I did it. Joyfully."

He has difficulty getting that last word out as his voice breaks. The memories are a flash flood that engulfs his emotions. He looks away to compose himself.

I pause, waiting out of respect, lots of it.

The memories subside. All that's past now. He's alone and Natasha is in good hands, but different hands.

He picks up the thread. "I'm noticing she doesn't need me anymore, because she's got her friends there. Now, I'm feeling I'm being kicked aside. It's a funny feeling, but a good one.

"This is now her life. She loves it."

* * *

Only when I ask does he talk about Natalie's mother, his only daughter. As with all parents whose child goes astray, he feels some guilt.

"I wasn't really here for my granddaughter that much—I mean for my daughter, excuse me.

"She started messing around with marijuana. Then, that led off to other things. Next thing you know, she comes home, she's pregnant. That's where my granddaughter came from."

It's an unfortunate story you have heard before: The girl got ensnared by drugs, got pregnant, was beaten up while carrying the baby, the child was born, was taken away by the court, and was due to be up for adoption when the grandparents stepped in and became appointed guardians.

Natasha today has very little contact with her mother. "Maybe once or twice a year, that's about it," Cliff says.

Have you ever talked it out with your daughter?

"Oh, yeah, a lot of times. We've talked it out. She has regrets. Yes, she does. She has a lot of regrets."

* * *

Cliff spent decades as an ironworker, which sounds challenging enough at sea level. He, however, often did his work hundreds of feet in the heavens, and closer to heaven than a sane person would want to get, at least for now. That's the opinion of this mild (and sensible) acrophobiac.

He worked on the Coronado Bridge and many high-rises in San Diego and throughout the West. He says the highest he ever worked was on an 1,800-foot broadcast tower in Walnut Grove, Calif., near Stockton.

You were strapped in, right?

"Strapped in to what? You're on a tower. You're going straight up on the outside, and you're just climbing on the iron as you go up. When you get up there, you just hook yourself up."

That gives me the chills.

He was amazed to be talking to such a wuss. "Really? To get to the top of buildings, we used to ride the pill. The pill is like a big ball on the end of a crane. You get on, cross your legs, and hold on. Then, up you go."

That didn't bother you?

"No. Why?"

You're a madman.

He laughs. "Well, you're going to die some time. Might as well die having fun doing what you do. To me, that was fun."

You've probably seen guys take the plunge, right?

The amusement came out of the topic and his voice slowed. "Back in '76 I was working on the Encina Power Station in Carlsbad. We were working on that tall smokestack—you can see it from the freeway.

"I was on the ground crew hooking things up to go up to the work site. Well, something happened, one of the cables on the crane snapped and it buckled and fell. Six men were killed.

"I was right there standing next to it as it was coming down. I went over there. I got my torch and cut the iron to get the bodies out."

* * *

The flinty guys he lived his life around would shake their heads in wonderment at his routine in taking care of Natasha.

"They'd ask, 'Do you clean the house and everything?' I says, 'Yeah.' They were amazed. 'Really? You don't have a woman now to do it for you?' I says, "No. I take care of my grand-daughter. I do all that kind of stuff.' 'Man,' they'd say, 'there's no way in hell I'd be doing that.' They'd tell me that all the time.

'You actually change a woman's Kotex? Oh, yuck. Man, you're nuts. Why don't you get somebody else to do it?' I say, 'Because she's my granddaughter .'"

* * *

Natasha knows the comfort of being all-in loved by her grandfather who is like crème brulee—sweet, once you break through the crust.

Cliff, has it occurred to you that very few men would or could do what you've done through the years?

"I don't know. I never thought of it."

Cliff Steagall is tough, as leather is tough. He is soft, as love is soft. He is a man, as a man is meant to be.

San Diego Union-Tribune, January 16, 2017

A dream dies alongside the road

Rachel Anne Morrison   **"Chip" Stockmeyer**

I t's Friday evening, March 28, 2014, and two lives are about to collide.

And shatter.

Rachel Anne Morrison is dining at Jake's in Del Mar. Christopher "Chip" Stockmeyer is drinking at a bar in Encinitas, six miles to the north.

Rachel is a Ph.D. student at Scripps Institute of Oceanography, San Diego. A 27-year-old native of Massachusetts, she is considered a scholar of great promise and a popular and admired member of that scientific community.

Stockmeyer, 41, is a construction manager living in La Jolla who this very morning signed his divorce papers, and whose son has leukemia, a condition that Stockmeyer has made it his mission to help overcome.

Rachel's dinner companion is Rebecca Williams, 31, the wife of Rachel's colleague at Scripps, project scientist Gareth (sic) Williams, Ph.D., 34. The two women share a love of long distance running.

They're discussing a chapter for Rachel's doctoral dissertation on results from a field trip she'd done in the South Pacific looking at the effects of fishing on coral reefs. No doubt the two are also talking about running and the guys in their lives.

Rachel is preparing to run the Boston Marathon alongside her father in three weeks. She is also engaged to marry. A young achiever with her plate full of delicious entrees.

Stockmeyer starts by drinking beer with some buddies, but as the evening wears on they depart for home. He stays, drinking alone. He wanders down the street to a second bar and switches to the hard stuff. He drinks and half-watches TV, still alone.

Rachel and Rebecca linger at their table. They each have one glass of wine during the evening. Rebecca gets a call from Gareth who was going to join them but is briefly delayed by work. The women decide to walk the half-mile to the Williamses' house.

At about 10 p.m., Rebecca and Rachel pay their bill and leave. So does Stockmeyer.

They are 15 minutes from each other.

The women stroll eastward down the curve of Coast Boulevard, a residential street that crosses the main road, Camino Del Mar, a quarter-mile south of Dog Beach. At about 10:15 they come to the intersection. There is a crosswalk protected by stop signs in both directions. The speed limit is 30 mph. Traffic is light as they look both ways. To the north, toward Encinitas, they see headlights quite a ways down the road. They make that everyday pedestrian mental computation—distance of cars, speed limit, crosswalk, stop signs—and then start to cross the street with Rebecca a half-step ahead.

Suddenly! With a freezing shock, monster headlights leap upon them, hot and bright as the sun. No time to fear. No time to scream. No time to pray.

Rebecca manages a small jump and feels a rush of air pressure as the car passes inches from her. She sees Rachel thrown into the air like a flimsy doll. Deputies later say she was thrown about 120 feet across the road. They calculate the car's speed as 60 mph.

* * *

Gareth is driving home when he sees people gathered and cars pulled over along Camino Del Mar, very close to his house. As he pulls to the side, tension boils in his mind as he fears something has happened to his wife or friend. No concrete reason to think that, but no one can outthink a premonition.

"I caught a glimpse of somebody lying on the ground, then I saw my wife standing on the side of the road. That was when I realized that it had to be Rachel on the ground. I quickly checked that Rebecca was okay. She was being held by a neighbor and beset by shock. She just said, 'They didn't stop. Rachel's been hit by a car.'

"I ran to Rachel. There was a gentleman trying to perform CPR. I have training, so I took over and quickly realized that she had been hit extremely hard. I could tell just from starting chest compressions that she was completely fractured everywhere. I tried to deliver the first breath and found her lungs were flooded with blood.

"She wasn't responding. I had to try to clean her airway and deliver another breath, but she already had refilled. She had huge internal hemorrhaging."

Deputies and an ambulance arrive, take charge, and rush Rachel to the emergency room. Gareth learned later that a medical team worked on her for 45 minutes, but he believes she was dead shortly after impact. The cause was a broken neck at the top of the spine and also at the bottom of the brain stem.

* * *

Rachel has been gone almost a year as Gareth sits at a family room table talking about his friend. He's tall and slim with burnished red hair. His soft Oxfordian English does not hide his emotion. The night we are here to discuss will never gray out in his memory.

It is difficult for him to talk about the killing of Rachel. The terrible event was unspeakable. His wife, Rebecca, who lived through it, needs to leave it that way—unspeakable—as do Rachel's parents.

Gareth is an understated man not given to gushing. "We sometimes try to glorify victims, but she was one of the nicest people I've ever met; very personable and a great communicator. Rachel was going to become somebody who could inspire the public to care about marine conservation; a public face for science.

"It was never about Rachel. Even the Boston Marathon she was training for. Even that was not for her. She knew her dad wanted to run a marathon with his daughter."

(Her father, John Morrison, completed the 2014 marathon—alone, but thinking of his daughter every step.)

When the news of the hit-and-run reached campus, Gareth says Scripps Institute put the school on pause and arranged a memorial service for Rachel.

"I have never seen such an outpouring of grief and love," he says. "It reminded everybody that Rachel was a beautiful person."

A website recorded the feelings of those who attended and contributed to her memory:

> "Rachel was as driven, tenacious, brilliant as a scientist as she was humble, kind, funny and generous as a person. I was lucky to have known her. Rest in peace, sweet Rachel."—Michael Navarro, friend and colleague.

> "I promise that Rachel's life, her passion for marine science and ocean conservation, her legacy as a generous

and giving friend, will live on here in my lab…We love you, Rachel." —Professor Jennifer Smith.

Then, of course, we have those fancifully named website-reader comments that spare not wrath and spare not words for the man who killed Rachel:

"What a son of a bitch. I hope they throw the book at him, actually, the whole library."—Nite shade

"I hope they take him to the courthouse steps and hang him high."—Sirdork.

* * *

Deputies going over the crime scene quickly come upon an Audi hood emblem and a license plate broken off during impact.

For investigators, it was evidence under the Christmas tree. Within an hour or so, they are ringing Stockmeyer's doorbell. He answers in a haze. He is reported to have told deputies that he "may have hit something," but isn't sure. He denies being aware of hitting Rachel. He says he just wanted to get home and go to sleep.

Stockmeyer is given a field sobriety test which he fails. He is then arrested. His blood is drawn several hours later. The Sheriff's Department calculates that at the time of the crash, his blood alcohol was 0.24, three times the legal limit.

The front end of Stockmeyer's Audi is badly dented and the driver's side windshield is shattered; not just spider-webbed, but smashed in a way that leaves visibility a guesswork.

Gareth Williams isn't buying Stockmeyer's story for one minute that he wasn't aware he hit Rachel.

"The airbag had deployed, his windshield was smashed. He would have had to drive 12 miles to his apartment with his head out the side window. To do that would take calculated decisions. From the moment Stockmeyer struck Rachel, it became 100 percent about self-preservation."

Prosecutor Keith Watanabe says, "He would have had to know he was in a crash. This was a callous disregard for the victim's life."

Gareth says, "I was always brought up to face your actions and be a man about it. He was a coward. I don't have respect for cowards.

"At the time I was extremely angry, now I just feel sad that he left my friend on the side of the road to die."

* * *

In his whole life, Christopher "Chip" Stockmeyer had never been told he was a bad man, much less a killer. Did he drink too much? Yes. But a killer? My God!

But here he sits in the prisoner's dock behind a wall of glass in Judge Michael Popkins' Vista courtroom on this day of June 20, 2014. He is facing a group of people seated a few feet away in the spectator section who loathe him. He has pleaded guilty to killing a person they loved. He broke her neck. His weapon was a car of almost two tons driven at high speed. His motive? None. He was deeply drunk.

The judge is about to sentence him to a prison term of 11 years—6 years for gross vehicular manslaughter while intoxicated, and 5 years for hit and run.

But first, Stockmeyer wants to speak. He stands up behind the glass. He glances out and sees eight stone-faced persons rising with him in unison. They each hold a photo of a pretty, smiling young woman: Rachel Anne Morrison, the daughter-sister-fiancé whose life he took.

Stockmeyer has a sheet of paper to read from, but as he starts, he begins to sob. As best he can, he begins: "To Rachel, her family, and my own family: I am eternally sorry for what I have done. I am horrified that my unintentional actions caused this absolutely horrible tragedy....I took Rachel away. I am repentant to God. I will think about Rachel every day....There is a black hole on my soul."

* * *

It's now eight months later and Stockmeyer walks into the interview with the carriage of the purposeful businessman he had been for a couple of decades. At age 42, he's trim and fit, and offers a firm handshake with a smile and direct look. He's dressed in blue pants and shirt.

Those are survival skills. The blue clothing is prison issue. He's just another inmate at Chino state prison, but he's trying to make the best of it. He's obviously bright and a crisp speaker. He's motivated to get out of this place as soon as possible.

He's approaching his sentence almost like a business plan. It's for 11 years, but by law he'll be released in October 2019. He's already climbed to the top of the inmate heap. He's been given a job as a mental health clerk, and is trying to get assigned to the fire camp. If he succeeds, he might be eligible for release in early 2018.

If the prison were filled with inmates like him, it would only need maybe two or three guards. He will be a model prisoner and give absolutely no trouble.

The only bars that give him trouble also have stools.

Coming in, he was terrified at all the horror stories he heard about prison. "I've seen some stuff that I didn't want to see, that I didn't want to know about. I've seen some bad fights. I saw a guy hang himself. You know, you're housed with uneducated, drug-addled thugs."

He says he's learned to avoid the racial gangs and the bad guys by developing an antenna for their scams and staying aloof without offending.

He shares a tiny cell with a lifer-burglar he gets along with. He's burrowed in. This is a resourceful man.

* * *

Stockmeyer says he's never gotten mixed up with street drugs, but he more than made up for it with liquor. He started drinking at

16, and was probably a functional alcoholic early on: Not the type
that craved a drink, but one that couldn't turn a drink down.

What's Stockmeyer's version of what happened that night?
(He doesn't have to ask, "What night?")

"I was meeting a couple of other guys there (in the first bar).
They soon left and went home to their wives. So, why didn't I just
leave with them, and say I don't need to be here any longer?

"I was drinking beer at the first place. When I got to the second
place, I started drinking cocktails. From there, I remember waking
up at my house with knocking on the door. And in between, I
really have no idea."

You don't remember a thing?

"I get like little snippets. Like, I think I can remember something wrong with the windshield of my car."

It was smashed. How did you see out of it?

"I have no idea. Driving blind, I guess. Then, if that's the case,
and I was that drunk, how did I even get to my car? Somehow, I
(found it) and started it. And when the cops got to my house, the
car was parked in my spot. I mean, my spot's not easy to get into.
So how did I do all that?"

You told deputies you thought maybe you hit something.

"I know. When they interviewed me, I was half asleep. I was
disoriented. I think I was still partially drunk. I remember them
asking questions, but I couldn't tell you what the questions were. I
couldn't tell you what my answers were. I could have said a lot of
things. I don't know how much of (what I said) was really true and
accurate or not. I had no idea there was a victim. I thought maybe
I had hit, like, a tree, or hit a—I just didn't know. All I knew was
I had been out drinking, and I was (now) home."

* * *

He doesn't back away from what he did, at least up to the
impact. He recalls that sentencing hearing in court: "They (the
family) all got up and said something. They called me a murderer,

called me a monster. And in that moment, yeah, I was a monster."

Do you feel you've gotten to know Rachel?

"I pray for her every day. I think I know her spiritually. It was a loving, promising person whose life I took."

Does Rachel ever visit you at night?

"When I talk to God, she's there."

Does she ever talk to you?

"No."

Can you see her face?

"I don't see her face, except for what I saw in the courtroom. I could see the portrait they were holding up. She was a bright light in the world that I took out, out of a stupid, ignorant act of my own. And there's nothing I can do to change it. I will get another chance, you know, but she won't. So I have to do something with my life."

Do you sleep well?

"No."

I say to him: You don't act like you've got the burden of a woman's death on your heart.

"I don't show how I feel. In here, you don't dare walk around depressed or sad. It'd be a sign of weakness."

* * *

Stockmeyer has two sons, both under 10. The oldest boy has had a tough battle with leukemia and is now in remission. Stockmeyer's absence from his son in this time of need is a tooth-ache in his soul. When the diagnosis was first made, he jumped in and helped raise money to fight the disease. He can barely finish a paragraph without mentioning his sons.

Both boys now visit him regularly. He tells me he hasn't talked to them yet about why he is here and not at home because he doesn't think they're totally aware of it yet.

As he tells me this, I think—Don't kid yourself.

When he was drinking in those Encinitas bars before the crime, he had that day received his divorce papers. It since has become final, but the woman who left him still has a hold on his heart. In conversation, he repeatedly refers to her as "my wife," though she is now his ex.

You still have fond feelings for your ex-wife.

"Oh, yeah. I love her, for sure."

But she's gone.

"Yeah, she's moved on to another guy."

He says, candidly, "My wife leaving me wasn't just because I was drinking too much. There was a lot of—there was just anger, there was depression, there was neglect, there was stupidity, there was dishonesty."

You know, some will say, "Why are you writing about this son of a bitch?"

"I know that. I might be asking the same," he says, nodding.

The Morrison family is suing him in civil court for a lot of money, but he's not worried about it because, he says, "I don't have any money. I'm in debt up to my eyeballs." Obviously, his insurance company will be the main target.

When he's released, Stockmeyer should be in better shape to fit back into society than many of his fellow inmates, many of whom have absolutely no chance of ever getting a meaningful job again.

In three or four years, Stockmeyer will be on the street in his mid-40s with a felony record. Not much call for that in the want ads. He has a college degree and a successful record in construction management, not huge but solid. He says he made $120,000 the last year he was working. Also, the construction business across the board is not known to be socially sensitive, so he should find it more conducive to easing back in. He agrees that is true. He also has a myriad of contacts.

On the other hand, it's a business known for fellows who are well practiced in bending an elbow, so he's concerned about its effect on his sobriety.

* * *

Stockmeyer is a strange fit for a felon. Until a year ago, he was a hard working, son loving, all-around hail-fellow-well-met. The character recommendations that were given the court on his behalf would fill a book. If he were your neighbor, you'd help him hang Christmas lights. But all of that has to be put on hold. For the next few years he's a convict serving time for a foul deed. He drank and drove and killed and ran.

There's a saying in prison that everyone is innocent, and everyone lies. Well, Stockmeyer says he's guilty. The fact is, he didn't have a lot of choice but to plead guilty, but, nevertheless, he has faced up to it, at least up to the crash. After that, there's an argument.

* * *

On any night on San Diego County roads a variation of this story could be repeated many times when the bars close and the neon goes dark. The roulette ball just happened to land on Stockmeyer's number. But the ball never stops spinning.

To those who swallow hard and think—"I could be Stockmeyer"…

Well, listen to yourself.

Christopher Stockmeyer alone knows the depth of his remorse. We can hope that he keeps his vow and overcomes alcoholism, and when he returns to his sons and to society, he will be a voice for sobriety. His life will go on.

Rachel Anne Morrison's will not.

She's gone.

San Diego Union-Tribune, March 15, 2015

Store helper is happy
with 'her 'normal'

Bobbi Schneider

So, I'm in the canned vegetable aisle of Ralph's in Encinitas, looking for tomato paste, the little can. Down the aisle pushing a wide broom comes this short lady. She smiles at everyone and maneuvers patiently around shopping carts, excusing herself as she goes. Then she bumps into mine. We talk.

She's Bobbi Schneider, and she's as open as a Kansas wheat field. She likes her job and finds it challenging. Bobbi says she's 40, which surprises me. I tell her she looks 10 years younger. (No, really. I don't just say that to women, not always.)

And yes, she has a disability. "Kinda slow," is how she puts it. In our conversation, kept brief because she has work to do, it's clear she's not used to people asking her about herself. However, she's pleased by the attention; it's something new.

I'm not surprised to find her here in this aisle. I've noticed large grocers often hire the mentally challenged for jobs at a doable level. They'll get well-earned points for that in corporate heaven, if there is one.

An hour later, my wife, Kathy, and I head for the Soup Plantation across the way with Bobbi as our guest.

* * *

There are navel-gazers in academe who don't have Bobbi
Schneider's introspection. She looks at you squarely, answers
every question directly, tells the truth and appreciates your interest.
Professionals who charge $200 per hour to eyeball you across a
mahogany desk could learn from Bobbi.

(I notice my tendency to think of this middle-aged woman as a
"girl." That may just be me, but I suspect not. Anyway, it's dispar-
aging and I silently vow to brush my mind of it.)

Bobbi was raised in Arizona and came here a couple of years
ago at the urging of two women cousins with whom she remains
close. Sadly, the same does not seem true of her parents back in
Arizona.

What exactly is your disability, Bobbi?

"'I'm not exactly sure. I learn slower than other people. My mom
calls it "M-R," which is mentally retarded, but I really don't know."

Does MR bother you?

"A little bit. I'd rather just be like normal people. I can do
everything that normal people do. I take care of my house. I can
cook. I like to make spaghetti. It's easy. And tacos."

Bobbi does not want to be rich, beautiful or successful. She
wants to be normal—a more laudable ambition.

Did you ever ask your mother why you're slow?

"I don't think I ever did. Sometimes I wonder."

A disability agency in Arizona once classified her as higher
functioning, which she defines proudly as, "Higher functioning,
like normal people."

Do you sometimes regret being disabled?

"Maybe a little bit. But I can learn like normal people."

Those who are disabled, as Bobbi is, though in her case only
moderately, often show impressive resourcefulness. She has an
I-Phone. (I have a hoary flip-top.) She is active on Facebook.
(myself, I have an account, but I misplaced the password.) She
knows her way around on city buses. (If I were to board one, I'd be
lost until I heard, "Next stop, Yuma.")

She spends time with her cousins, but doesn't have hardly any girl friends, because they like to gossip about guys, babies and fashion. She wouldn't have much to contribute. Bobbi would like more friends but is uncertain how to go about it.

She spends her evenings and weekends playing on her keyboard, watching TV and reading. She is currently reading "Island of the Blue Dolphins," of which she says, "I think it's a kid's book, a teenage book."

Where do you think you'll be in 10 years?

"I don't know. I don't think about that too often. I bet you anything I'll be right here."

"Do you ever ask for a little more responsibility?

"I've never said that. I don't even think to say that."

When you were growing up, did kids tease you?

"A lot of kids teased me. They called me a retard a lot. I didn't like it. I don't like getting teased. If I told them to please stop, they wouldn't. That made me sad."

(Bobbi becomes "sad," not "mad." Mad is for normal folk.)

Any teasing as an adult?

There's a couple people that teased me. One called me—it's kind of bad—"

Go ahead.

"He called me the B-word. That just hurt really bad."

If it makes you feel better, Bobbi, a lot of women you would admire are called that. It's usually out of anger or spite. Whoever called you that was not making fun of your disability.

"Really? OK."

I ask Bobbi if she is returning to Arizona for Thanksgiving or Christmas to see her family, and she hesitates. She doesn't know, but says the decision will be hers.

She anticipates my next question: "I'm really not very close to them."

Do you hear from them very often? Do they call you?

"Not too often. Sometimes I talk to my mom on Facebook."

They weren't mean to you, were they?

"I don't think my mom was."

What was the problem? Because you're disabled?

"I think so, yeah. I'm just not close to them."

Here's an example of Bobbi's maturity and bigness: Her first few months in San Diego she lived with a cousin and her husband. However, as time went on, the home got smaller and smaller, so Bobbi looked for a different place to live. She says she "totally" understands the couple's desire to have a more private life, and harbors zero ill will about it. Classy.

* * *

Fifteen months ago, Bobbi went online and applied for a "courtesy clerk" job at Ralph's because she worked five years in the same job at Fry's in Tucson, and both are Kroger companies.

She works 16-20 hours per week doing a variety of jobs: sweeping, retrieving carts, bagging groceries, helping customers to their cars, and doing price checks. She thinks her pay is $8.25.

That income gives a modest lift to her Social Security SSI. And though her one-bedroom apartment in a Carlsbad complex rents for only $725, she still survives on thin gruel. She rides the bus and has no credit card, and that keeps her expenses down.

She's been on her own since high school, but this is the first time she's had her own place sans roommates. In the past, she's also held minimum-wage jobs as a teacher's aide at a pre-school center and for a Tucson Dunkin' Donuts.

The Dunkin' Donuts gig taught her one downside of the workplace. They closed the store without notice, and she found out about it only when she showed up for work. She thinks they paid her.

Bobbi is more interesting than many Mensa geniuses and has greater job-satisfaction than many MBAs. She makes prudent money decisions that bankruptcy lawyers will say is beyond the common sense of some rich people. She'd like to be understood, like most of us, but it's something she's rarely experienced. She also finds some ordinary thought processes puzzling, which she freely admits, but she soldiers on.

She enjoys her job, though its twists and turns can be burdensome. Once in a while she gets confused by the rules of bagging—don't bag food with household chemicals, and don't make the bags too heavy. But with a little patience from the cashier, it works out OK.

Do you sometimes restock items on the shelves?

"Sometimes I have to do stuff like that. Sometimes that's hard."

Going to the shelves to price-check an item, however, can be a swim upstream in a spring flood. Though she gets the job done, it's like a physics exam for a sophomore.

Retrieving carts from the parking lot is the job she would like to avoid, but doesn't, nor does she complain, though multiple carts can be a heavy push.

Bobbi says she doesn't have a boyfriend, and I ask if she'd like one.

"I don't know. There's times that I do, and there's times I don't." She says she had a couple of dates in her 20s.

Did that work out OK?

"Not really."

Why not?

"Because it didn't."

Check that off, huh?

"Yeah."

* * *

Bobbi Schneider is an exemplar of open-mindedness and a generous spirit. Often, we shy away from the disabled, not knowing what to say or afraid of saying the wrong thing; maybe thinking they're society's wallflowers and not worth the time. The feeling often is—different isn't a bad thing, but it's also not comfortable.

Listen to Bobbi. She doesn't resent others' better fortune. Honesty is at the top of her values list and vanity near the bottom. It would be a good thing if some of Bobbi's "normal" could be more normal for the rest of us.

I'll use the "G" word just one time—You go, girl!

San Diego Union-Tribune, December 1, 2014

'Things were fine until those guys came'

Richard Carrico

Long forgotten, but once located under what is now a busy Sorrento Valley freeway interchange in North County San Diego, the village of Ystagua was home to 200 Kumeyaay Native Americans. Richard Carrico of San Diego State University tells us how they lived when the Spanish came in the late 1700s.

Ystagua was peaceful, and prosperous within its environment, something like Tahiti might have been before the famous "Bounty" and other ships dropped anchor.

Then, some strange men dressed in iron showed up on an otherwise ordinary day in 1769 and made it the day Ystagua began to die.

(The phonetic pronunciation of Ystagua is "estawa.")

Perhaps they were first seen by women looking up from weaving yucca leaves or leaching acorns. Or maybe they were seen by men returning from clamming at the nearby lagoon. One glance, and the Kumeyaay were unimpressed.

What they saw walking into the town clearing were a group of men recently off of a many-months journey in vermin infested, tiny ships. They were dressed in ragged, filthy clothing. Most were sick. Some carried death for the Indians hidden in their bodies.

They commonly had scurvy, a disease that imprints its repulsive marks on the body like a tattoo. They stank, they had ulcerated faces, their teeth were falling out. And when they opened their mouths the odor was a dog's breath wind in the faces of the scrubbed-clean Indians.

Hello, Spaniards.

Despite common belief, the Kumeyaay were not blown away by these strange "gods" (hardly) from, maybe, heaven. They knew about Europeans who had first come to the Southwest in the mid-1500s with Coronado. The explorer did not make it to what is now San Diego, but word gets around.

* * *

Richard Carrico is author of "Strangers in a Stolen Land," about San Diego's indigenous peoples (Amazon).

He says the Kumeyaay were not an excitable people. They just studied these guys and figured things out.

"They liked their ships with the big sails. They thought those were bad-ass canoes, and they liked their leather jackets, and they liked their metal swords, and they really liked cloth because they didn't see a lot of that. The fire-sticks really impressed the villagers. They thought those were fearsome.

"But the Kumeyaay processed information in very interesting ways—Of course, you have a fire stick because you've got a big canoe, and you also have cloth and leather. So, of course, you have a fire stick. "

Stands to reason.

They didn't figure on the smallpox, the measles and the sexually-transmitted diseases. Those you couldn't see, but they were already on the way.

The Spaniards, led by Gaspar de Portola, had landed in San Diego Bay earlier that year. It took a while to make the 20 miles up to Ystagua. There were other villages to visit along the way. However, they finally heard that the springs a couple of hours up the road offered fresh water and were near a nice town called Ystagua.

* * *

The Kumeyaay were a "stone-age people."

Some people wince at that, but it only means they did not work metal for weapons or utensils.

Without metal devices, they lusted after the knives and tools the Spaniards dangled in addition to the cloth. In return, they offered pots, baskets, and—hallelujah!—fresh fish, meat and vegetables.

Pretty soon, though, with the trading done, the Kumeyaay, being jealous of their space, began to look at these pigpen guys and think, "Are we done here?"

The Indians quickly figured out these guys weren't going home. They were like brothers-in-law on the couch.

The seeds of conflict were planted early.

* * *

Now, you start with young guys fresh ("fresh"—perhaps not the right word) off a long voyage; what do you think might be on their minds (to say it delicately)?

Right. Carrico sets the stage: "You're a Spanish soldier, and you see this topless woman. She seems to be flaunting herself, and she's giggling, and she seems to like you. You give her some trade beads and—this is not going to go well."

Because the Spanish came from a more buttoned-down society, they misread the sexual innocence of the Kumeyaay women who had no fear of sexual abuse and rape. When that changed, hatred was born.

There was an early outbreak of violence as the Indians attacked Father Junipero Serra and his party at the foot of Presidio Hill near present-day Old Town shortly after they arrived. The attack was thwarted, but it portended things to come. Soon after, Serra moved on north.

Then the Europeans' diseases hit and the Indians sickened and many died. Not knowing about contagion, the despairing and confused people didn't know where to turn.

Carrico says, "I believe the Kumeyaay started thinking that maybe their god, their spirit, wasn't as strong as they thought, and the European god was stronger. When the Spaniards built a modest mission on the site of the later historic one, they now had a place where the Indians probably assumed the new god lived.

Carrico surmises that the Spanish priests fed on that fear, and offered a solution: Convert. "They said, 'You're being punished for not believing. That's why you're all dying.' Very clever. Of course, they may have even believed that themselves."

The Kumeyaay probably figured—What've we got to lose? If becoming Catholic is what will save us, well then, that's what we better do.

Conversion became sort of a spiritual insurance policy. Doubtful that many saw the light because of the writings of St. Augustine. Based on mission records, an estimated 15 percent were baptized.

It didn't take long for the invaders' influence to be felt. Carrico describes what developed in the villages and around the newly-established San Diego mission where some Kumeyaay moved.

"In Ystagua, you'd see some women and men wearing glass trade beads from the mission. You'd probably see people with syphilis on their face. You'd see cornfields, beanfields and other crops that the Spaniards taught them to grow. You're going to see a lot of sick people, and you're going to see a smaller population."

A large majority of the Indians didn't buy what the priests were selling. They just hung back and watched their culture start to come apart.

The name Kumeyaay has had an interesting journey of its own. Back in 1700, if you were to ask a resident of Ystagua what he called his people, he would have blinked in confusion, as though, "Do we need a name?" Then, if pressed, he would have said he was of the town of Ystagua, which means "worm's home." Pressed to go more broadly than the village, he would have said—nothing.

The Spaniards, who went around the world passing out names, called them "Diegueno," or "the native people of San Diego." And that is the name that stuck for about 200 years.

Finally, in the birth of Native American nationalism of the 1970s, it was decided to seek a more authentic name than the one given by the white man. So, they came up with one that had long slumbered in their lore and that meant "people of the coast." Thus, Kumeyaay.

The Indians who lived in the Oceanside area were given the name Luiseno, "people of San Luis Rey," and they still seem content with that.

Personal names had a method and a rationale. Carrico gives an example: "One young woman was listed in mission baptism records as "Sinkusiyaay Sichac." Sin being woman and kusiyaay meaning healer. So her given name was healer woman. Her clan name was Sichac which was an important clan. Sichac means owl. So she was healer woman of the owl clan."

The priests brought Old World discipline to the mission and that was a shock. (Remember, back home, these were the days of the Inquisition where you could get yourself burned at the stake for praying to the same god in the wrong way.)

The priests were kinder than the military over at the Presidio, but that was of small comfort. Whippings were the common physical punishment. Now, that may have been business as usual for a tough sailor on a galleon, but to a placid native, it was shocking abuse.

The Spaniards, who would need little excuse to start a fight, looked down on the Indians. Carrico says, "I read those early records of Father Serra and talk was of the Kumeyaay being a docile people. They used phrases like, 'War is almost unknown to them.'

"They had a rude surprise when the Indians rebelled and rose up in 1775. After deciding that the priest, Father Jaime, was a demon, they sacked the mission in San Diego and burned it to the ground. They killed him and two other people."

The Spanish came close to abandoning this area, but Serra returned a year later, rebuilt the mission, and began a placating regime that was kinder toward the Kumeyaay.

Altogether, Serra spent only 87 days in this area.

Carrico says, "They took a George W. Bush approach of being a kinder conservative, and made attempts to make amends. It worked to a degree."

Life gradually returned to normal in Ystagua and among the Indians of this area. Or should we say abnormal? Of course, if abnormal is the status quo long enough, it becomes normal.

Carrico says a visit to Ystagua 100 years later, in 1800, would find only about 100 people, a decline of half since 1700. It would be something akin to an American rust-belt city of today compared to 50 years ago.

Disease would have done its dirty work. Carrico says, "When I dug at the Mission San Diego in 1989, we found the first case of congenital syphilis on an Indian. It was a little boy who died when he was 8 years old. His body was ravaged by syphilis. He died around 1800. He was born with syphilis. His bone structure was just porous."

Carrico points out a less obvious effect of syphilis, a disease that often leaves the victim sterile. He says that if a normal woman had been fertile in that time, she probably would have had 3 girls, of which 2 would survive. But this infected woman had none.

However, if those 2 girls (who were never born) would have each had 2 girls of their own, and if those girls and each girl of succeeding generations would have had 2 girls...you can do the math to realize how that one disease denied normal population growth to the entire Kumeyaay people.

The European domination and cultural foothold gradually became a full-body embrace, and the once reassuring hum of Kumeyaay life gradually faded, and finally could barely be heard.

San Diego Union-Tribune, October 31, 2016

The 'king of the hills' lived high, died low

Charlie as the noose descends

Charlie's gang; he is seated center, top car

I t was the morning of April 19, 1928, and Charlie Birger, the most celebrated bootlegger-gangster in Southern Illinois, whose colorful exploits had fascinated the nation, became the last man publicly hanged in the state.

* * *

The small boy gripped his father's hand and remained quiet, carefully emulating the 100 men who spoke hushed, short words all around him. Outside the fence behind him, 5,000 other men, women and children waited in the same churchlike solemnity. A few intrepid boys had climbed high into trees to watch. It was the largest public gathering in anyone's memory in the southern Illinois community of Benton. About 29 feet away, just beyond the broad shoulders rising all around him, Gene Powell, age 9, could see the scaffold and the slack noose that dangled from a thick cross beam, swaying softly in the breeze.

Suddenly, the heavy door to the jail right behind the scaffold swung open, creaking in the silence, and a small group of grim men filed out. The boy's eyes were first drawn to a man reading from a book, slow and sorrowful, but they quickly shifted to a dapper man in his mid-40s whose hands were cuffed in front of him. Charlie Birger was handsome in a youngish, open-faced way. Although of medium height, he loomed large here, as he would have in any crowd. He was dressed in a new gray suit, and he nodded and smiled to acquaintances as he started to walk. "Hey, Bill, how you doin'?" It was obvious that he liked people, and many liked him.

Underneath the open scaffold, Birger passed the wicker casket that would soon hold his body. He spat into it just before he started up the 13 stairs to the platform. He took them steadily, appearing more relaxed than those who watched.

On the platform, Birger stood erect and patient as he waited. He chatted with lawmen while the rabbi intoned divine reassurance. The hangman asked if he wanted a black hood or a white one. The condemned man, an enemy of the Ku Klux Klan, laughed and said black. "I've never liked Klux colors."

Just before the hood was put in place, he was asked if he wanted to say any last words. He looked at the faces below him, many of which were sad, even tearful. He looked beyond to the blue sky latticed by the spring buds of a giant oak tree and felt the breeze for the last time. "It's a beautiful world," he said in a clear voice. Reporters from Chicago, St. Louis and the wire services strained to hear his words and scribbled them down.

There were about 10 minutes remaining of his life before the appointed hour of 10 a.m., but he stepped directly onto the trap-door. "Let's get on with it. I forgive everybody." The hangman made a last check of the thick noose pulled snug just under the left ear, then solemnly nodded to Sheriff Jim Pritchard, who stood at the back of the platform with his hand on the lever.

The lawman tightened his jaw and his grip, hesitated, then yanked. The trap clattered open and Birger plunged through.

Gene Powell blinked as the hooded man suddenly disappeared amid the jarring noise of the trap door. Outside the barrier, another boy, Johnnie Warren, 6, was looking through a crack in the thrown-together fence. All he could see was the open area beneath the scaffold. Suddenly, he was startled as his view was filled by a hooded body falling into the space.

"Birger Dies Smiling," blared the local newspaper. Birger was dead, but his legend took on new life.

* * *

They were called the "Roaring '20s," but the meaning of the phrase varied widely, from the roar of the crowd cheering Red Grange and Charles Lindbergh to the roar of machine guns as gangsters fought for the spoils of Prohibition. It was a period of wealth for a few, and the illusion of wealth for many as inflated stock certificates papered over reality. However, in rural America the Depression came a decade early, as farmers confronted a postwar grain glut.

In southern Illinois it was worse, because the land there lacked the fertility of the glacial soil deposited in the northern part of the state. So, as much of the country enjoyed the economic boom, the miners and dirt farmers in Little Egypt read their Sears catalogs and nursed grudges against the merchants and bankers. They were themselves rigidly conventional, but many secretly admired anyone bold enough to challenge authority.

Shachna Itzik Birger, born in 1880 in Russia according to his military record, came to America in the wave of Eastern European Jews that stepped off the boat at the end of the 19th Century. According to Birger biographer Gary DeNeal, author of "Knight of Another Sort," Birger's family moved to St. Louis. Later, he joined the U.S. Cavalry and served in the Far West, where he also became a cowboy skilled at breaking wild horses.

After the Army, Birger returned to the rough area of East St. Louis and for about eight years knocked about in obscure jobs. He

was 5 feet 8 and wiry, handsome and pleasant enough if he was
getting his way. But "if you pushed Charlie, you had somebody to
fight," says Benton businessman and historian Bob Rea.

In 1913, Birger and the first of his four wives moved to the
coal mining town of Ledford in Saline County, where opportunity
beckoned. The community was "dry" by local option, and Birger
set himself up as a small-time bootlegger and pimp.

Saline was one of three adjoining counties—Franklin and
Williamson were the others—that were unique in having a
booming mining industry and a multi-ethnic population. The
counties shared a history of labor and criminal violence, both
before and after the Charlie Birger era, earning the region the title
"Bloody Williamson."

Birger forged an informal business alliance between the hill
people who manufactured much of his booze in deep-woods stills
and the miners who consumed most of it. Local police were not
especially eager to enforce the law and arrest the bootleggers,
who often were neighbors and boys they had gone to school with.
Chances were, the cops also drank the stuff themselves. They let
the lawbreakers slide, then took the inevitable step into complicity
by accepting small bribes.

While the mine owners enjoyed the lake breezes along the
Gold Coast in Chicago, their workers lived in a landscape of
poverty, sickness and a black dust that coated everything—
clothes, skin and lungs. Into this wide prairie of poverty came
a golden opportunity for the enterprising Birger as the calendar
turned into 1920. The anti-liquor forces in America had finally
won their century-long social and political battle with the enact-
ment of Prohibition. The celebrations of the "drys" were matched
by those of the bootleggers, who knew that the taste for their
product could not be legislated away and that boom times were
ahead.

Birger's rise to prominence in Bloody Williamson was due to
both his winning personality and his ruthlessness with rivals. He
was a showman who loved acclaim perhaps more than a dollar.

He resembled cowboy movie star Tom Mix, and he played on that, dressing in Western clothes and bragging about his background as a cavalryman and breaker of wild horses.

He played community benefactor by giving small amounts of money to the needy and making his autos and telephone available to people who could never afford such luxuries themselves. Such small acts of generosity made a big impression in a poor community in the '20s and contributed to Birger's legend as a kind of Robin Hood. Kids flocked to him as he gave them the Pied Piper treatment with liberal bribes of ice cream and watermelon. A favorite flourish was to go to a schoolyard and toss dimes to the children, many of whom could otherwise go a year without seeing a 10-cent piece.

Birger's darker side also emerged: He killed at least two men in those early years, both small-time thugs, and in each case successfully pleaded self-defense. "Charlie was a one-trick dog," Rea says. "Whenever he wanted to kill someone, he would antagonize him until the fellow publicly threatened Charlie. Then he could claim self-defense when it came time to do the killing."

As Birger himself blandly explained, "I never killed anyone who didn't deserve killing."

DeNeal, the man who has studied Birger the most, can offer no explanation for a man who could kill one day and buy ice cream for children the next. "His charities were extensive, and it wasn't just PR. He really liked people and wanted to be liked. He really did kill people, and he really did help the poor." However contradictory it seemed, Birger's behavior gave him the useful reputation of being a good man to know, but a bad man to cross.

As Birger thrived in his bootlegging business, a growing number of the established community seethed. They were the people who had fostered Prohibition in the first place, mainly churchgoers and their preachers. Aghast at the unchecked crime and violence in their midst, and not knowing which policemen they could trust, they turned elsewhere for help—to the Ku Klux Klan and a man eager to lead them named S. Glenn Young.

The Klan in those days was especially strong in southern Illinois, where many sought its help because they distrusted the authorities. In the Bloody Williamson area, the issue was not racism or nativism— Klan staples—but law and order. By advertising itself as the champion of decency, the Klan was able to recruit hundreds of followers and make itself acceptable to thousands more who otherwise would have spurned them as "white trash."

Young often appeared in public in riding pants and boots, pearl-handled six-shooters strapped to his thighs and a submachine gun cradled in his arms. He was a former Prohibition agent who was fired and prosecuted for various abuses, including killing a man. In 1923 Young was looking for a cause, and the respectables of the Bloody Williamson counties were looking for a crusader. They hired Young, and in December the night rides began.

Klan raiders led by Young smashed in front doors all over the area and ripped up floorboards looking for illegal hooch. Using phony warrants, the Klansmen arrested dozens of minor offenders.

Birger was Young's main target, and the bootlegger and his allies fought back, supported by the people who were abused by the raids. While driving to East St. Louis in 1924, Young was ambushed by gunfire in Washington County. His wife was left blind by the attack, but Young was only slightly wounded.

His luck ran out on the night of Jan. 24, 1925, when he and some of his cronies gathered in the European Hotel in Herrin, and Ora Thomas, a lawman with connections to Birger, walked in. A fusillade of gunshots followed, and in seconds two of Young's bodyguards were dead and archenemies Young and Thomas lay dying.

Despite Young's long list of enemies, his funeral was one of the largest public events ever held in any small town. An estimated 75,000 filed by as he lay in state and up to 40,000 thronged around the Baptist church where his funeral took place. For years afterward, his foes used his tombstone in a Herrin cemetery for target practice, and to this day it sits pocked with bullet holes.

Reeling from the death of its leader, the Klan tried to use the event to rally more support, but then came the bloody showdown of April 13, 1926, Election Day in Herrin. Polling places were packed with contentious poll watchers for both sides—the Klan and their church allies and the bootleggers and other anti-Klan citizens.

In one place, John Smith, a Klan leader, challenged several Catholic voters, including a nun of 20 years' residence. Word of the dispute spread through the town, outraging residents, and Smith went into hiding in a local garage. A carload of anti-Klan gangsters soon found him and opened fire on the building, setting off a gunfight that ended only after 20 National Guardsmen arrived from Carbondale and deployed around the garage with fixed bayonets. Another gunfight that day resulted in three dead from each side. Even though the battle seems to have been a standoff, the bloodshed further demoralized Klan members and the organization was finished in the area. Hundreds of charges against the victims of their raids were dismissed.

Birger, the Klan's main target, had won, aided by the great number of local people in the three counties who—for a mix of motives, some of them noble—sided with the gangsters to rid themselves of hoods, raids and burning crosses.

As Birger prospered, he set his sights on expansion. He cut a deal with another bootlegger gang in the area, led by Carl Shelton and his two brothers. In 1925 the two gangs shook hands on joint operations, including driving imported liquor up from Florida, much of which would end up in Chicago. They also agreed to split illegal slot machine proceeds. Perhaps predictably, the partnership soon fell apart, most likely because of cheating in the collecting, counting and divvying-up of the gambling loot. "One thing gangsters know is each other. Enough said," says history professor John Simon of Southern Illinois University.

Whatever the cause, the two gangs opened another chapter in the Bloody Williamson saga by going to war in the summer of 1926, complete with armored vehicles and an air force. DeNeal describes the Shelton gang's "tank" in one incident that targeted

Birger gangster Art Newman and his wife: "A 2 1/2-ton truck came rumbling toward them. Protruding from the circular steel tank on the back was an assembly of weapons, all of them aimed at the couple. In the ensuing gunfire, 25 bullets tore through the car, but only Bessie was wounded, and she only slightly."

A month later, Shelton hired a plane to fly over a Birger hideout called Shady Rest and drop sticks of dynamite on the sturdy log structure. No damage was done, but it made history by becoming the first known aerial bombing in the U.S.

The war lasted six months and left as many as two dozen dead, by DeNeal's estimate. Bodies were found lying in culverts, floating in streams and sitting in cars alongside the road.

Birger was remarkably open about his criminal exploits. During the gang war, he reportedly asked that a message be read over local radio that the public was safe because only other gangsters would be killed. He publicly boasted of his intent to kill a Shelton ally named Joe Adams, who also happened to be the mayor of West City, near Benton.

In December 1926, Birger paid $50 each to two teenage orphans who were gang hangers-on, Harry and Elmo Thomasson, and sent them to kill Adams—which they did, on the front porch of his home in daylight. Two weeks later, Birger was arrested in connection with the slaying.

Had he been accused only of the Adams murder, he might have gotten off or at worst been given a long sentence. However, three days before Birger was jailed for the Adams killing, his gangsters abducted and killed a state policeman and his wife. The policeman was alleged to have been involved in the local rackets, but his wife, a well-liked schoolteacher who was rumored to be pregnant, was viewed by the public as innocent of anything her husband might have been involved in.

Birger had finally exceeded the limits of public tolerance, and suddenly Robin Hood didn't seem so romantic. Public opinion turned against him and officials, fearing a lynching, transferred him to another jail.

When Birger's trial opened on July 6, reporters for big-city newspapers showed up and focused the nation's attention on the gangster and the goings-on in Bloody Williamson. Birger's lawyers played for sympathy by having his two elementary-school daughters in attendance. But when Harry Thomasson dramatically appeared and testified that he and his brother killed Joe Adams on orders of Birger, the gangster knew what was about to happen.

"I'm done," he predicted to reporters. Eighteen days later, Birger, Newman and a third man were convicted, but only Birger was given the death penalty.

His lawyers tried various appeals, but nothing worked. Finally, in desperation, they requested a sanity hearing. Birger, however, hurt his own faint hopes by joking during the hearing that he should be buried in a Catholic cemetery because the devil would never look for a Jew there.

After that, Birger could only watch and listen to the hammering as the scaffold that would hang him was finished in the jail yard just beneath his window.

Three-quarters of a century later, Charlie Birger's death is an image that the young witnesses, Gene Powell and Johnnie Warren, now struggle as old men to retain in their memories, like the flickerings of an old movie. But his mystique endures in the region's lore.

Birger was buried in a Jewish cemetery in University City outside St. Louis. The faith he abandoned had reclaimed him in the end.

Chicago Tribune Magazine, October 7, 2001

Recalling the glory, and a baseball fight to remember

Kurt Bevacqua

It's Oct. 10, 1984, San Diego Jack Murphy Stadium in Mission Valley, almost 58,000 fans in attendance. It's the second game of the World Series, fifth inning. Right-hander Dan Petry is on the mound for the Detroit Tigers protecting a 3-2 lead with two Padres on base, one out. A right-handed batter is up. Petry is known for a wicked slider, a pitch that breaks down and away from a right-handed hitter; a hybrid of a curve and fastball.

He throws the first pitch, a slider, for ball one. The second pitch is also a slider for strike one. The third pitch is again a slider, and it's high in the strike zone. The batter swings and connects, although he gets under it a bit. He sees that the ball's flight is high and deep to left field. It's either a home run or a long out. He begins to fast-jog down the line, watching…

The home run hitter, Kurt Bevacqua, is 37 years old, a journeyman nearing career's end, and batting as a designated hitter. He's a utility player widely acclaimed in the game as a great bench jockey, skilled at throwing opponents off stride with his mouth.

Just a couple of steps from first base, he sees the ball fall into the left field stands. He slows to a trot, throwing a fist in the air as thousands cheer, but he doesn't hear them. His mind goes numb until he sees third base coach Ozzie Virgil cheering him on home. Then it occurs to him: This is the World Series and I'm a hero.

He played in the majors for 15 years as a versatile fill-in player who could play five positions and with a Pete Rose élan for the game. It's an unusually long career for any player, least of all a utility player. As it might be said, he did not reach his potential, he exceeded it.

So long as memory serves, Bevacqua will relive that moment. So long as he lives in Carlsbad, Padre fans will remind him.

That moment and a crude encounter with Dodger manager Tom Lasorda two years earlier have enshrined him in Padre folklore. That was when he called Lasorda a fat little Italian, and the pugnacious Dodger—no mean man himself with a needle—responded with what has become one of the all-time favorite baseball Youtube videos. The one where he says, "BeVACqua? That (a bleep with muscle) couldn't hit water if he fell out of a boat. If I was pitching (against him) I'd send a limousine to make sure that that (bleeps to the fourth power) got to the ballpark on time."

That war of the two hall of fame taunters was epic—Godzilla meets King Kong. Your teenage kids may have already seen the video, but you may not want your grandmother to.

Bevacqua was and is a throwback kind of guy. Today, he's a homebody businessman of 65 who could comfortably pass for 55, with a five-child family and in the after-market car business. Interviewing him, I wait and overhear while he takes a couple of business calls. He's a straight-ahead guy. Boom, boom, boom. It's push ahead and get the deal done. He probably doesn't catch a lot of Jane Austen movies.

It was Bevacqua's gift for agitation that made him a prime mover in one of baseball's entertainment highlights earlier in that championship '84 season.

* * *

It's Aug. 12th. The Padres, in the midst of their pennant fight, are playing the Braves in Atlanta. Alan Wiggins, who vexed the

Braves with multiple hits last night, is the leadoff hitter. On the mound is Pascual Perez, a pretty good pitcher known for being rail skinny and behavior so bizarre he would have been kicked out of Jerry Springer's green room. Perez's intent is to punish Wiggins for his earlier success. Bavacqua is on the bench.

The first pitch hits Wiggins in the back. He glares theatrically out at the mound and the Padre bench comes to the dugout steps, muttering with palpable menace. Then, in that same half-inning, sitting in the dugout and plotting revenge are Padres catcher Terry Kennedy and pitcher Ed Whitson. In baseball, tit-for-tat is a commandment written in fire across the sky.

Kennedy and Whitson are planning a reprisal hit on Braves' lead-off hitter Jerry Royster. As they talk, edging into the conversation is the ever-helpful Bevacqua who points out that Royster is an innocent; the one to nail is Perez. Upon further reflection, that makes sense to Kennedy and Whitson.

Move to the third inning: Perez is batting for the first time. Whitson throws at him and Perez pirouettes out of the way. The umpire then warns both managers of expulsion for them and their pitchers if the bean-balls continue.

Back on the bench, Bevacqua, knowing that during a game manager Dick Williams has the snarl of two dogs with one bone, plays Iago to his boss' Othello and whispers in his ear of the evil ways of Braves pitchers and their conspiring teammates.

Williams, fuming, and anticipating his own ejection, names about three coaches as his successors, assuming that each, in turn, will join him and his pitchers in the showers. Then he stomps out and gestures to relief pitchers to start warming up: It's on.

Over the next five innings Padres pitchers play Perez for a piñata, but an elusive one. He comes to the plate the way a matador approaches the bull. Getting hit with a 90-mph fastball is less appealing than a root canal. Perez's objective is not to get a hit, but rather not to get hit. He looks out at the Padres pitcher who is fingering the ball and looking back at him with an expression that is either grim-faced or grinning. Both mean the same thing.

Several times the dugouts empty and stare-downs and brawls erupt around the field. Typically, a baseball melee is one of two things: a dance contest or a big pile with every player using his hands to cover his head. This is different—the swings are real, and guys who might normally, after the game, get together with beers and groupies are slugging each other. Braves outfielder Gerald Perry lands a nasty sucker punch on Tim Flannery. I'm sure it occurs to Flannery: Hey, this is supposed to be a baseball fight!

After several brawls and numerous ejections, the umpires finally restore order—for a while. Bevacqua tells what happened at the end: "So, in his fourth at bat, we finally hit Perez in the eighth inning, and we're thinking everything's done. But in the top of the ninth, we're at bat. They're changing pitchers. (Braves reliever) Donnie Moore is coming into the game, and Graig Nettles is the leadoff hitter. He sees Moore coming in, so he comes back to the dugout, and says, 'You guys better get ready.' What are you talking about? He says, 'I nailed Moore during the fight, and he knows it was me.' Sure enough, the first pitch hits Nettles right in the back, and here we go again." In the last brawl, Bevacqua is seen on tape swinging wildly, stirring a breeze in the warm Georgia air.

In this final round, Bevacqua confesses to an error in judgment. He says someone in the stands poured beer on him and he impulsively jumped the railing to go after him. Whereupon, "I went into the stands after the last fight, and that was kind of a mistake because I got it handed to me by four rednecks. My spikes slipped out from under me and I fell, and they were on top of me like snow in an avalanche. I got ejected then." For the night's fun, 13 were ejected and five fans arrested.

As do all fun things, the bean-brawl finally ended and left lots of fans with something to chortle about. It also left Bevacqua with a baseball story for the ages, and, as all baseball stories do, one that will undoubtedly improve with age.

San Diego Union-Tribune, August 27, 2012

Ruler of all he imagined

Emperor Joshua Norton

He owned San Francisco. With the self-assurance of his royal status, he strolled the streets of the crowded commercial district throughout the 1860s and '70s. He wore a tall beaver hat with a plume and rosette, dressed in a blue suit with tarnished gold-plate epaulettes, and carried both a cane and a tri-color umbrella. His oversized shoes were sensibly ventilated with holes to provide relief for his corns. On ceremonial occasions he would even wear a sword.

Celebrated though he was, it was only on the day that he, Joshua Abraham Norton, dropped dead of a stroke on a busy street corner that officials first entered his home. It was a 50-cent per night room at the Eureka Lodging House, and it was where he lived for 17 years.

The room was about ten feet by six feet. There they found a camp cot with crossed legs, one straight-back chair, and a pitcher and basin. Strewn about were proclamations, telegrams and pictures of other reigning monarchs, especially of his hoped-for consort, Queen Victoria. (If he had seen that dowager's picture, his intent must have been only for purposes of power consolidation.)

In his possession were $5.50 and mining stock certificates worthlessly proclaiming face value exceeding a million dollars. It was spectacularly downscale for a man who carried the weight of two nations on his shoulders.

Thus ended the reign of "Norton I, Dei Gratia, Emperor of the United States and Protector of Mexico" on January 8, 1880. Though some later called him "The Mad Monarch of America," they never did to his face. For over twenty years, the portly, fierce-eyed ruler patrolled the bustling, free-for-all city with shoulders stooped, hair sprouting from beneath his cap, and with a "rapt far-away gaze" most of the time. But Norton was not born to the purple. He started his San Francisco career as just another rich businessman.

Norton arrived in San Francisco from South Africa in 1849 as a 30-year-old successful merchant with a worth of $40,000. Little was known about him except that he had been born in Great Britain, probably London, and was Jewish. However, in the next four years, smart investing in real estate increased his fortune to about $250,000. He was a first-team player in a town where cornering a buck was the big game.

Then he got greedy. In December of 1852, a rice shortage caused the price to escalate from four cents per pound to thirty-seven cents. When a ship loaded with rice came into the harbor, Norton bought the entire shipment for twelve cents per pound, trying to corner the market. He was on the verge of cashing in when at least one more ship sailed in with her hold full of rice.

The price plummeted to three cents and Norton was ruined. Sketchy accounts attest that he tried to pay off his debts, but filed for bankruptcy in 1856. Then, after serving as a juror at a trial on Sept. 28, 1857, he abruptly disappeared. No one ever learned where.

In the next two years, San Francisco continued to be, well, San Francisco. The "easy riches" gold had already been plucked from the Sierra stream beds, but the city remained wide-open as a sanctuary from Victorian rectitude. Hustlers abounded, and bizarre characters were tolerated, even encouraged, and daily walked the streets giving unsquelched voice to their delusions. They were a promenade—George Washington the Second, the Great Unknown, the Guttersnipe, the Money King, and a quack peddler called the King of Pain.

Then, on Sept. 17, 1859, Norton reappeared and overshadowed them all. Dressed in an operetta-style uniform, he entered the office of the San Francisco Bulletin where he demanded publication of a proclamation which "…at the request of a large majority of the citizens of these United States," introduced himself as their emperor and demanded obedience.

The town loved it. Mark Twain, with an ever-open eye for affectionate instability, called him a "lovable old humbug" and is said to have patterned the King in *Huckleberry Finn* after him. His endearment to San Francisco said as much about the liberality of the city as it did about Norton. Robert Louis Stevenson, who traveled through San Francisco, wrote, "In what other city would a harmless madman…have been so fostered and encouraged?"

PROCLAMATION.

Norton I., *Dei Gratia*, Emperor of the United States and Protector of Mexico, being desirous of allaying the dissensions of party strife now existing within our realm, do hereby dissolve and abolish the Democratic and Republican parties, and also do hereby decree disfranchisement and imprisonment, for not more than ten nor less than five years, to all persons leading to any violation of this imperial decree.   Norton I.
Given at San Francisco, Cal., this 12th day of August, A.D. 1869.

San Francisco Herald
Friday, August 13, 1869

Norton issued proclamations, decrees, and imperiously gave his "patronage" in return for meals, uniforms, transportation, and free drinks— always in moderation. Merchants and bankers would redeem the fifty-cent "bonds" he had had printed. He was given a lifetime pass on the Central Pacific Railroad, and on those occasions when he visited the capital at Sacramento, he was given a special chair in the Senate chambers where he would sit for a while and take copious notes.

Herbert Asbury wrote in 1933: "He ate without paying at whatever restaurant, lunchroom, or saloon took his fancy; after he visited an establishment, the owners were permitted to post a sign: 'By Appointment to the Emperor, Norton I.' Invariably, these 'appointments' brought great business to the saloon or restaurant so graced."

The effect his business failure had in creating his addled state is not known, but biographer Allen Stanley Lane said in 1939, "There is no evidence that Norton revealed any striking erratic tendencies during his business career. He probably held in check any irrational whims. But being a proud and sensitive man, he suffered great mental torture over his misfortunes."

Psychiatrist Robert Solomon of San Diego recently undertook to put Norton on the couch from a distance of a century and a quarter. Based on the accounts left behind, the psychiatrist says we know he suffered a later-age-onset cataclysmic blow to his ego, was not violent, did not have a substance abuse problem, and had only a single primary delusion. Based on his behavior, Solomon discounts schizophrenia, bi-polar disorder and depression-caused psychosis.

Solomon thinks the stress of Norton losing all his assets pushed him into a relatively rare condition called a "delusional disorder of the grandiose type" which resulted in the emperor-imaginings that lasted more than two decades up to the time of his death.

The emperor was a proud man who bore the royal mantle easily. On one occasion, concerned about the fraying of his uniform, he proclaimed, "We, etc., have heard serious complaints from our adherents and all around that our imperial wardrobe is a national disgrace; and even His majesty the King of Pain has had his sympathy excited so far as to offer us a suit of clothing, which we have had a delicacy in not accepting. Therefore, we warn those whose duty it is to attend to these affairs that their scalps are in danger if our said word is unheeded."

The Board of Supervisors responded by buying him a new uniform and presented it to him in a city hall ceremony.

The emperor was arrested only once, in 1867 by a young deputy with more zeal than judgment who charged him with lunacy. However, the charge was quickly dropped by a judge with this explanation: "He had shed no blood, robbed no one, and despoiled no country, which is more than can be said of his fellows in that line."

Norton's name endures mainly because of his frequent proclamations which still ring with pomp, authority and righteous indignation. His language was officious, his topics timely, and his reach grandiose. The San Francisco newspapers vied to publish them.

In 1878, Anglophile Norton sent a cablegram to the Ameer of Afghanistan warning that fellow ruler about his supposed hostility toward Britain. "Norton I informs the Ameer that he (Norton) is dictator of the peace of Europe; that he will make it Mighty Warm for him if he precipitates a war." One can imagine the unknowing Ameer studying this threatening cable with knitted brow while sycophants cluster around pledging till-death support.

As evidenced by the endangered Ameer and Emperor Maximillian of Mexico whom he threatened with execution, Norton could be harsh in his pronouncements. On another occasion, in 1860, he abolished Congress; he then ordered Gen. Winfield Scott to use troops to scatter the politicians when they disobeyed.

He also fired President Abraham Lincoln. He ordered the assets of the First National Bank of San Francisco seized in 1869 because it refused to cash his $100 check, and thereby jeopardized the financial stability of the realm.

In 1872, he endeared himself to San Franciscans forever by decreeing, "Whoever after due and proper warning shall be heard to utter the abominable word "Frisco," which has no linguistic or other warrant, shall be deemed guilty of a High Misdemeanor, and shall pay into the Imperial Treasury as penalty the sum of twenty-five dollars."

Perhaps the main reason Norton was cut an extra length of slack by even the more sober-minded citizens was that he was a kindly man who threatened no one. In one account, he rose to the defense of an unpopular minority:

"During one of the typical anti-Chinese demonstrations so common at the time... (he) sensing the dangerously heated tone of (the) meeting, Norton is reported to have stood up before the group, bowed his head and begun reciting the Lord's Prayer. Within a few minutes the agitators retreated in shame without putting any of their threats into cruel action." Norton also proved a seer by calling for a suspension bridge between San Francisco and Oakland, a good half century before the Bay Bridge made it to the drawing boards.

Despite all the bizarre characters running around the city, Norton's preeminence among them was unchallenged until he had to share public attention with a couple of street curs. Bummer and Lazarus were a team of mutts who for a few years in the mid-'60s also worked their way into the hearts of the city and formed an ad-hoc scrounging team with Norton.

Lane described Bummer as, "A small black mongrel with white spots. He had an unusually projecting lower jaw, and teeth too prominent for his lips to cover. The result was a permanent sardonic grin, whether awake or asleep. He had no owner and wanted none. He became the city's champion rat killer." Lazarus, Lane said, was smaller and subordinate to Bummer. "He was a "thin, mangy, yellowish-black cur."

Although neither the dogs nor Norton made ownership claims on the other, the emperor and the canines became linked in the public perception as they made the rounds together seeking out free saloon lunches, and were content spending long hours patrolling the streets in each others' company.

The *Daily Alta California* in 1861 explained that the dogs had teamed up when Bummer rescued Lazarus from a dog-fight mauling. "The poor cur had one of his legs half bitten through, and having limped upon the sidewalk, he proceeded to scrape an acquaintance with his deliverer, Bummer, who thenceforth took him under his special protection. Every night since, the two dogs have slept coiled up together, close to some doorway—Bummer always giving the lame cur the inside berth, and trying to keep him as warm as possible."

The same newspaper the next year added to the dogs' legend: "Yesterday afternoon, the notorious curs, Bummer and Lazarus, chased a runaway team up Clay Street, one taking one side of the thoroughfare, and one the other. On reaching the corner of Kearny, Bummer rushed in front of the horse and held him at bay until a man came up and caught the team, Lazarus being on hand to check any further advance. These dogs may now be considered in the employ of the city, and of course are exempt from taxation."

An assistant dogcatcher once seized Lazarus, only to be mobbed by a crowd. Money was raised immediately for the dog's release, and neither dog was ever arrested again. The Board of Supervisors exempted them from a strict ordinance that banned all dogs downtown without a leash or muzzle, and allowed them to run free, which the dogs had intended to do anyway.

Lazarus died of poison in 1863. Bummer was stomped to death by a drunk in 1865. Not everyone can get into the spirit.

They collected enough money to dignify Norton's body with new clothes and a rosewood casket. His funeral cortege was two miles long, and crowd estimates ranged as high as 30,000. He was buried by the Masons, and without the traditional tallit burial shawl of his Judaism.

In 1934, his body was moved to Woodlawn Cemetery in suburban Colma where the grave today has a handsome stone marker which gives his full title as he believed it to be. The Emperor has been adopted by the Gay and Lesbian Coalition of San Francisco who each March hold an Emperor Norton celebration that draws several hundred. A biker club and E. Clampus Vitus, the club of partying history buffs, also show up annually to celebrate his colorful life.

If it had been Norton's misfortune to sink into mental illness in about any other American city in the mid-nineteenth century, he probably would have been locked-up. Remember, this was the same period in which the Abraham Lincoln's depressed widow was institutionalized briefly by court order.

And if Norton wandered the streets of San Francisco today, he'd be lost in the crowd of thousands of homeless who've taken refuge in that tolerant city, many of them far crazier than the emperor, and none of them nearly so humorous.

Norton did not see himself a victim and the society he lived in didn't either. If his delusions of grandeur represented the groping of his mind to recapture the public esteem he had known before his bankruptcy, then he succeeded by grace of the forbearance and sense of humor of San Francisco. The city foreshadowed its present self, and showed that even in the Victorian Era it was possible to hang loose.

As a historical figure His Majesty is a winner. After all, other than the yearned-for Victoria, how many other rulers of the time can you name?

American History Magazine, 2004

A cop who wouldn't quit finds justice

Helena Greenwood   **David Paul Frediani**

L ate in January, 2001, as the small audience in the Vista courtroom north of San Diego awaits the judge's entry, all eyes seek out the defendant's table, then turn away, but always turn back. It is where David Paul Frediani sits, accused of a murder that few even remember. His gaze is fixed straight ahead, seemingly locked on the state seal above the judge's empty bench. Surely, one thinks, he knows that everyone sitting behind him is staring at the back of his head.

He is tall and sinewy, a swarthy man of 46 who looks younger, with a physique even younger yet. He is an MBA who served as a financial analyst with Pacific Bell in San Francisco at the time of his arrest. In a different setting he might be considered handsome, but here he looks hard and mean, the type of man who always wins a staredown. Longtime acquaintances know little about him, but one thing is said time and again—he has problems with women.

Little notice is taken of someone nearby, a person easily overlooked and unbothered by it. She is a grandmother and a country woman whose clothes probably come from discount stores so she can save for new furniture. Her words are soft and plain. Having struggled up from the lower middle class, she is not frightened by vulnerability. She's small, not much over 5 feet, with a blond pony tail, and she's not afraid to cry.

Even so, you don't want her tracking you. She is Laura Heilig, a 50-year-old homicide detective for the San Diego County Sheriff's Department. This is her case, and because she sits here, so does Frediani. She is the one who arrested him more than a year ago.

As the lead detective, Heilig sits next to the prosecutor, facing the same direction as Frediani. At the moment, the lawyers are elsewhere, so only the two of them are at the pushed-together tables, about 8 feet apart. While waiting for court to begin, she busies herself with small tasks while he just sits there.

They do not look at each other. However, she thinks of him constantly, because she is convinced that 16 years ago he broke into a woman's home and sexually molested her, and then returned a year later and murdered her to remove the threat of her testimony at his trial. The victim was a stranger. Her name was Helena Greenwood, a 35-year-old PhD biochemist who had emigrated from Britain. She was a tall, willowy woman whose friends say would thoughtlessly throw on designer clothes like items from a thrift shop.

As a leader in the exciting new field of medical DNA, she had more important things on her mind. Heilig knows the details. She has lived with them for many months. . . . On the morning of Aug. 22, 1985, after Greenwood's husband had left for work, the young scientist finished a final phone call, gathered up her work papers and, as the clock neared 9 a.m., started for the office. In the dense shrubbery outside, or perhaps hidden in the shadows of the high fence that surrounded the Del Mar house, a killer waited.

Alerted in the early afternoon by Helena's absence from work, her husband, Roger, drove home to check on her. After parking, he approached the solid-panel gate and pushed to gain entry. It wouldn't budge. He went off to the side to peer over to see what the obstruction was. He saw. It was Helena's body lying on her back at the base of the gate in the flaccid stillness of death. Homicide detectives investigated, but searching the scene proved fruitless.

The autopsy showed she had been strangled. Blood had flowed from scalp lacerations and was on her clothes and at the scene. She had fought hard. There were minute traces of blood under her torn fingernails, which the medical examiners scraped and clipped. Everything was saved and put in evidence containers. Police were certain—absolutely certain—who the killer was: her accused sex attacker, David Paul Frediani. However, though his alibi was weak, there was no evidence to tie him to the murder.

Months later, Frediani went on trial for the sex attack. Even though Helena was gone, a fingerprint he had left in her bedroom was enough to force him to plead no contest and serve three years in prison. After his release, he went back to his life in the Bay Area as a loner with few friends. He had been a prime suspect in other sex attacks before he went to prison but had no arrests following his release.

Over time, the murder file was routinely moved into archives, where it reposed along with 300 other unsolved homicides. Police gradually assumed—grudgingly—that Frediani was just another one to get away with murder. To those who knew the victim, grief slowly receded and life moved on. Remembrance of Helena took on the dull coloration of the long dead.

Since 1992, Heilig has been assigned to the homicide archives department, where she is on a team of four who look for justice beyond the cobwebs that time leaves behind. Her job involves going through old files and looking for cases that might be resurrected and—who knows?—even solved. The Greenwood file had become one of them.

In the archives, 300 human tragedies dating back to 1930 occupy shelves in silent indictment of this life and how it was taken from them. They are once-upon-a-time people who smile out of faded snapshots that lie atop yellowed reports that were obviously wrong or insufficient. Often, the detectives are the only people remaining who care about these victims, or even know they were ever on this Earth. The work they do is typically not dangerous, strenuous or fascinating. It's reading files. Then reading them again. And a third time.

With some of the later cases, witnesses are still alive and the puzzles are fresher. Heilig, for example, is currently working files that range from a 1976 case of two 12-year-old boys from the same school who were killed three months apart, to the 1989 rape-murder of an elderly woman who was stabbed to death with a screwdriver. This is work that needs to be left at the office.

The trial settles into the metronome of the prosecutor's persistent questioning. She is Valerie Summers, an organized, matter-of-fact woman whose evidence presses the breath out of Frediani's defense like the weight of stones. DNA experts place Frediani's blood at the scene to the statistical exclusion of anyone else in 2.3 quadrillion (23 zeros) people, which means that no one but Frediani, on Earth or in the solar system, could possibly match that blood.

Summers guides a crime-scene expert through a demonstration of how the murder unfolded, of how Helena was grabbed by the throat and steadily choked—for three to five minutes—until her brain shut down and her body died.

The expert, Rod Englert of Portland, Ore., dramatically reconstructs how desperately she fought for her life and managed to claw at him and get his blood under her nails and even on her clothing. He says that strangulation is the most intimate method of murder. It allows hate to flow through the fingers into the struggling body of the victim. Then, as though rage were not enough, he points to the photo of Helena lying dead and says that she did not fall into that flat position. She was posed. And then the killer took his bloody, gloved hands and placed them on her ankles and opened her legs as a parting insult. He pauses, and the courtroom silence seems to scream.

The time comes for Heilig to take the stand. She is led through her investigation, step by step. When asked to identify the man she arrested, she looks directly at Frediani. "That man, sitting on the end." He glares at her. Her testimony sounds routine because it is smothered in facts and dates and procedures carefully recited. There is far more in her head than she is asked to tell the jury.

It wasn't long into the new job before Heilig opened the Greenwood file; she well remembers the day she removed the color photo of the tall, slim woman lying in the dirt and stared at it. Her face is twisted to the side. Her half-opened eyes are without focus. The little things from her purse that tie us to the world—keys, coins, lipstick—lay strewn around her. Work papers with her blood on them have been scattered by the breeze. Near her head is a small carton of yogurt and a plastic spoon—lunch. She has been thrown away, discarded.

Heilig gradually became acquainted with the victim, who was her own age, a woman who had achieved what girls of their generation were often led to believe was out of reach. She became good friends with Helena's memory and thought of the sad reality of her dying savagely as a stranger in a foreign land. There had been little time to make friends, and after her widower died of cancer in 1999, no one in the world remained to mourn the dead woman except an elderly father in England.

In 1998, mindful of the steady advances that DNA science had made in criminal forensics, she and her teammates slowly started going through old cases that included blood evidence that might be tested. She remembered the Greenwood case. Working with her teammates and criminalist Mary Buglio, she sent the fingernails that had been ripped from Helena's struggling hands to a DNA lab in Northern California. Month after month passed with no results because archives cases were constantly pushed to the bottom of the priority list by current cases.

The delay may have been fortuitous, however, because at about the same time DNA science made a huge leap forward, resulting in a process called STR that allows more "markers" to emerge from evidence and thus gives a more definitive reading. If the evidence had been tested even a year sooner, it might have rendered insufficient results and would also have destroyed the blood particles. End result: Frediani might never have been identified.

Finally, the laboratory reported back that the evidence showed a second person's blood in addition to Helena's. Next, Heilig and Buglio requested a testing of Frediani's blood sample that the state had on file by virtue of him being a sex felon. It confirmed that it was Frediani's blood that had been left under Helena's fingernails.

Heilig remembers the day: "Mary came down with a big grin on her face carrying the lab results. She shouted, 'It's a match!' and we hugged and danced around like kids."

That Frediani was identified because of DNA, the science Helena's career was devoted to advancing, is an ugly irony. No one says "poetic justice," because there's no poetry in it, and justice can't restore her life.

On Dec. 15, 1999, in the early morning, Heilig and a group of backup police staked out a parked Lexus. They were in Burlingame, in the Bay Area, waiting for David Paul Frediani. When he casually approached his car to go to work, she walked up with handcuffs at the ready. "You are under arrest for the murder of Helena Greenwood."

"All color left his face," she said later in an interview. "He went pale white. He didn't say a word, just stared straight ahead."

* * *

Defense attorney David Bartick, an able lawyer by reputation, stands before a stonewall of evidence and gropes for cracks. He tries to counter the DNA experts with one of his own whose credentials pale beside those of the prosecution's. He tries to challenge the kit used in the tests. But when Summers draws out of the defense expert that the kit is widely accepted nationwide, including by the FBI, the argument is deflated. Bartick raises questions about mysterious witnesses and implies mishandled evidence. None of it seems to work. At one point, a journalist turns to a colleague and silently mouths, "O.J. won't work here." Later, an uninvolved defense lawyer described how his kind cope when confronting an apparent slam-dunk case. "You just tell yourself it's a long, drawn-out guilty plea," he said with a wan smile.

Toward the end, Bartick tries what has to be a desperation play. He calls the accused to the stand. Frediani cannot shed the imperiousness embedded in his personality. He had always maintained his innocence of the 1984 sexual attack and said he pleaded no contest just to get it over with. Now, Summers has the right to show that his motive for the murder was in trying to cover up that crime. She bores in with relish. This is personal. Her voice and body language intensify. She pounds Frediani with questions and backs him into a corner about that denial. "That wasn't true, was it?" Frediani is nervous and stammers slightly. "For purposes of these proceedings, I accept responsibility [for the sex attack]. What do you want from me?" he said, turning to the jury as he speaks.

She is 15 feet distant, but he knows she is right in his face. "I want the truth," she demands. "The truth is, you forced Dr. Helena Greenwood to orally copulate you. Isn't that true?" He has nowhere to go. His shoulders seem to sag. "Yes, that's true," he admits for the first time.

Later, Heilig said, "I cried, right there at the table, when he finally admitted that." In her closing argument, Summers points to Frediani and says to the jury, "That man came down and killed her, and as she lay there, you know what he did. He took his hands—the hands that had her life blood mixed with his guilty, vile blood—and he put them around her ankles . . . and he spread her legs as a final insult."

Late Monday afternoon, just over a week ago, the eight women and four men of the jury return with a verdict. Although one woman has slightly red eyes, the others are quiet, but not remorseful. Two men are smiling. As the clerk prepares to read the verdict, Frediani crosses his right leg over his knee and tries to appear unaffected. Only a frequent wetting of his lips reveals otherwise.

The verdict is what everyone knows is coming, but it still resounds in the quiet courtroom: "Guilty of murder in the first degree." The only sign of emotion is when Frediani's father closes his eyes and bows his head. His wife gently puts her hand on his leg. The old man's son is without expression. He must have known it was coming.

Early the next morning in homicide headquarters in San Diego, detectives walk into Heilig's desk area with coffee cups and big grins. Their hearty hugs, handshakes and praise reveal her popularity and the pride they take in her success.

"I guess it's time to go call Sydney," she says, referring to Helena's 88-year-old artist father, whose breaths can almost be counted, so close to death is he from cancer. He has told more than one person he wanted to live long enough to see justice done. One of Heilig's partners, Curt Goldberg, pulls a tissue from a box, hesitates, then pulls another. "You'll need these," he jokes kindly.

In a small room, Heilig calls the lengthy international number, waits, then speaks to the neighbor who is taking care of Helena's father. "How's Mr. Greenwood doing?. . . Oh, really?" Her voice drops. "I'm sorry. . . ." She is told that he is asleep, that he can no longer talk but seems to understand words spoken to him. Heilig asks that he be told that Helena's murderer "will never, ever get out of prison." She listens again, then says, "I personally believe God has allowed Mr. Greenwood to live this long so he would know of this." She provides details for a few minutes, then ends by saying, "Please tell him he is in my prayers."

David Paul Frediani will never give us the satisfaction of figuring him out. Inscrutability is his protection, and perhaps his revenge. All we really know from his past is that women are his chosen enemy. He even murdered one. But after he is sentenced in March and told he will never be free again, he will have many days to sit and think of the people who put him there—Mary Buglio, Valerie Summers, Laura Heilig and, yes, the one who marked him forever by fighting for her life, Helena Greenwood.

Eleven hours after Laura Heilig made her call, Sydney Greenwood died.

Los Angeles Times, February 7, 2001

Homeless youth struggled to escape despair

S tudent janitor Michael Gaulden drags his mop, pail and broom into the boys' bathroom at San Diego High School. The floor and walls are spotted with feces, maybe deliberately, he thinks. The floor has small puddles of urine. His job is to clean it all up.

Michael Gaulden

As he works, a crowd of boys watches him and cracks jokes. "Shit boy," they call him, but that's not the word they use. With every insult, they hoot and guffaw and slap hands at their cleverness. They take cell phone photos of him scrubbing.

He's black and so are they. So what? Bullies don't care about victims' color, only that they're vulnerable.

The janitor is only a kid, but he's doing work most men would turn away from. However, he has no choice. If he does not, his mother and sister will suffer even more.

He keeps his head down and scrubs. Does he block out the abuse and dream of a better tomorrow? No. That's for kids from wealthy Del Mar. But down where he lives most fantasies come from doing dope.

He has been placed in the job by a San Diego Workforce Partnership youth program. He works it as diligently as a CEO, minus the golf, because it might be a way to help him escape the life he's been trapped in.

It does. He catches a break and is able to surf that high tide Shakespeare tells us about, and goes on to win a college scholarship, and with the help of every part-time job he could hustle, he walked away with an honest-to-goodness degree from UCLA.

Now 23, Michael now works as a career counselor at San Diego's inner city Monarch School.

* * *

By the calendar, the incident in the bathroom happened 7 years ago. But in the memory of Michael Gaulden, it happened yesterday, because it left an indelible imprint.

Today, Michael works with kids whom the education system either forgot or can't find. He's a happy-faced, buff and confident guy in trendy clothes who works to keep today's kids from having to mop a bathroom.

I don't personally care for the word ghetto. It just leaves a metallic taste on my tongue. However, the area just south of downtown is a ghetto; not a racial one, but a ghetto of despair. The "drive-bys" that happen here are not gang shootings, but the indifference of society that speeds by on the interstate without seeing the unsmiling people just beyond the off-ramp.

There was no shortcut for Michael. He only briefly knew a real home until he leased a one-bedroom apartment of his own in Spring Valley last year.

He spent his years from 7 to 17 living in a car; over-night stops at cheap motels, often in a room with several strangers; in rescue shelters until being "timed out"; briefly, in juvenile hall; in a randomly pitched tent; and worst, on the streets—literally, the cold, unforgiving concrete of some of the most dangerous, grimiest cracked sidewalks of San Diego.

Michael shared the ratty cushions of beat-up cars with a mother who was frequently ill, sometimes desperately, and a sister one year older who suffered seizures.

His father? Yes, his father...Michael's father is in prison serving a very long stretch for murder. Michael has not seen him since he was 12. Michael's grandfather was murdered in prison, and his father before him.

Considering the family history, if this story were about Michael following in those footsteps and being in prison himself, we both would say, "I'm not surprised." Statistics don't always lie.

But he didn't. Michael is not in prison. So how in the world did that happen?

Persistent sickness will drag anyone down, but when you're homeless, disease tends to dig in and take root. Michael's mother managed to keep them in an apartment until he was 7, but lost her job because of illness. From that point, for the small family "address unknown" was where they lived.

It was a quiet day on the trolley and 16-year-old Michael should have been relaxed. But you can't, not where he lives. Danger might be hiding in the quiet. Ever watchful, he notices five young men "eyeballing" him. All are strangers. He averts his eyes to signal he wishes no trouble.

He should have known better than to rely on wishes with those guys.

Michael says, "They walk up to me, and it's like, 'Who are you? Where you from?' I'm, like, 'Michael, and I don't gang bang at all.'

"Next thing, one guy hits me on one side of the head. Another guy hits me on the other side. They start stomping me out. I try to cover up, and they pull my hands apart to hit me in the face."

With a concussion and a face covered in blood, the police take him off the trolley. Before they can sort things out, the five hoodlums disappear. One of the cops concludes, 'Oh, it's gang related.'

Why did they jump you?

"No reason," he says. "They're angry. They're poor. They have to lash out and I was the victim that day. That wasn't the first time something like that happened, but that time made me understand, 'I won't survive this too much longer if I stay here.'"

Were you wearing blue or red (gang colors) or something?

"No. I was careful not to. You stick to dull colors when you're in the inner city, but, as I found out, it doesn't matter what you wear. It doesn't matter if you're not a gang-banger. It doesn't matter, any of that. If they want to attack you, they're going to attack you."

You were 16. Weren't you thinking, I'm going to get a gun and my homies and come back here and waste those punks?

"I never thought like that. I didn't even have money to get a gun. All my cousins were in gangs, and doing stuff like shooting people. But I wasn't, because that comes with death. That comes with jail. I've seen it my whole life. Most of my family members are drug addicts, drug dealers, or criminals. That wasn't the way for me. But choosing to be different leaves you susceptible to being alone in the inner city."

When Michael's mother was well enough to work—any work she could get— they might scrape together $300 to $500 for an old car, mainly to sleep in. It was a whole lot better than the street. If they were lucky, the car might be a "donator."

"Living that way, it was terrible. I hated it. I keep the mental picture with me everywhere I go because I hated it. I'll never forget. I'll never let myself forget having police bother you, having people look at you like you were less than an animal."

When their mother was frequently in the hospital, Michael and his sister were left to fend for themselves, sometimes at age 11 or 12. They turned to begging, or to use the dressed-up word—panhandling.

"I was great at it. I had enough practice. It's not as easy as you would think. People just don't hand out money, but when you're a kid and they can look into your eyes and look at your clothes and see the desolation, they're bound to give you a dollar every now and then. We lived on that.

"You survive. That's when you meet people. You got homies, or you couch surf. You try to do whatever you got to do. Sometimes you tag along with groups of people; one of them's getting a motel that night and you just crash along with them. You eat at the charity places.

"We just had to do what we had to do until mom got out of the hospital, and then we went back in the car."

The obvious question is why he didn't turn to Child Protective Services, or why CPS didn't seek him and his sister out. He makes it clear that in the black underclass, CPS was something to be avoided, almost feared.

"It's the system. I've seen many kids get lost in it. All my cousins were in foster care. The system, it's flawed. It's looked upon negatively in the inner city. They don't want CPS to come and take kids because they never seem to get back to their parents. It breaks apart families."

Were you ever in foster care?

"Never."

Michael says that on the rare occasions he would be in a nice neighborhood, he would feel like a ghost, just roaming around, an invisible being until he got in someone's way or tried to touch something.

"It was terrible. There's a shelter called YWCA El Cortez, and the historic hotel called El Cortez is nearby. From my window in the shelter, me and my sister, we could see the lights from that other El Cortez. I was like, 'One day we'll be on the other side.'"

* * *

Nights in San Diego are mild. That's experience when you're in a heated house and your car's windshield doesn't frost overnight. But when you're homeless, the cold laughs at rag-tag coats, and the wind makes you cower in a doorway.

Let's briefly visit Michael in his Ford-junker bedroom. He has to watch his mother in pain with no meds, trying to find comfort in the back seat of the old car; his sister is complaining that he ate the last of the Doritos; he's trying to stay warm with his legs contorted under the steering wheel and watching a rat forage under a streetlight.

In his life, laughter has no humor, the future tells lies, and something called hope is turning tricks in a hourly-rate motel down the street. A prayer is not for world peace, but that there will be enough for seconds at the shelter soup line.

* * *

Then, 16-year-old Michael went to a different sort of "other side." He stood lookout while his cousins broke into a house. The teen burglars ran afoul of a Neighborhood Watch sentinel and were grabbed by police. He was given probation as a first offender.

Being a teenager is synonymous with a lot of boiling, bubbling emotions, anger being a geyser. For a homeless kid, it's Old Faithful.

Tell us about anger, Michael.

"I was mad at everyone for a while. I mean, you're a teenager. However, people who have a volatile personality, they can go off the tracks. I've seen it. I've seen friends with those temper problems turn into killers; shooting at kids. I've witnessed a lot of things in my time. I was mad because I was like—This is just so unfair. I didn't do anything wrong to be in this situation.

"Counselors are supposed to talk to you and they want you to understand. I had a counselor and she was like, 'Do you trust me?' I'm like, 'No, I don't trust you.' They want you to get them to trust you, except when you get up to stretch or something, they jump out of their skin and grab their purse."

However, the most demanding question was one he eventually had to ask himself: "Am I a criminal?"

Over time, he answered that question, and loudly, in the negative.

We started this story telling about when Michael, a homeless teenager, suffered ridicule and bullying by working as a student janitor. But that was a good thing—the job, I mean.

The money he earned enabled him to help put his mother and older sister, both in bad health, in public housing where they still reside. It was the first honest-to-goodness home they could call their own in years.

We can ask why there are not more Michael Gauldens who can climb out of poverty and be useful citizens.

That's a fair question, but then we should also ask—Why are there so many who have to try?

San Diego Union-Tribune, February 8, 2016

Out of war's violence came gentleness

Bob Farner shows his medals

If you pass on the street an old man with white hair, flannel shirt and worn blue jeans moving gingerly with the ache of arthritis and a heart prone to misbehavior, you normally just glance and walk on by. But if that man is Bob Farner, stop and look back at a real life Dr. Dolittle who is also a war hero. And that's using "hero" in its true meaning. Stored at home are a Silver Star, a Bronze Star, and two Purple Hearts.

The man comes across as anything but heroic. He's a big, bluff fellow with no pretention. He lives in a small home in Vista, California that could use a younger man's upkeep. It has a large, bare backyard filled with ducks, fangy mongrels, an emu that eats romaine lettuce—no iceberg, thank you—and even a big alligator, all of which are still alive because he took them in. And, except for the gator who is not welcome in polite society outside his pen, the animals walk free. The ducks waddle by a streetwise German Shepard as though they're first cousins.

Farner, 89, is a retired Marine non-com who later became a school janitor. He may be the only old-time sergeant who says gosh, golly and darn.

He is a retired self-taught wildlife rehabilitator who has the touch to sooth the savage beast, or at least the predator with jaws that throw sparks when they snap. He once had a mountain lion and a coyote that couldn't be returned to the wild, so he used them to educate school kids. The cougar would ride in the front seat with him; the coyote would sleep at night on his bed. (Be careful rolling over, Bob.)

But hidden far deeper than his friendly face are memories of brutality, barbed wire and the stare of death. Back in the spring of 1942 he was burrowed into the undergrowth on Corregidor, the small Manila Bay island where Gen. MacArthur and a bedraggled group of Marines, Filipino soldiers, and medical personnel, including many nurses, were besieged by attacking Japanese troops. He served as a guard for MacArthur there and admired the general, a feeling probably in the minority among the troops.

Farner was an aggressive fighter. After the enemy managed the short trip across the water to Corregidor, he and others were waiting. "I loved my B.A.R.," he says at the memory of his heavy, large-caliber automatic weapon.

"I truly did love that rifle. But one time when I let loose, a Marine near me shouted, 'Get away from us with that damn thing. It's drawing all the fire.' I remember when this Jap tank came through the undergrowth, and this officer was standing in the turret. I got a good bead, and pop!" WWII Marines still tend to be unapologetic; it's not hatred, just the way it was.

Farner says the troops had plenty of fight, but not much medicine, ammunition, food or hope. He speaks with frustration still to this day of a low-flying enemy plane that circled his position as the time of surrender neared. "I ran to a .50 caliber and swung it around and pointed it, then the plate fell out. Darn it! I coulda got that plane." The gun had been made useless, probably to keep it out of enemy hands.

At the U.S. surrender, on April 9, when a captain carrying a white flag told Farner to turn in his B.A.R., he protested in astonishment. "Hell, we can beat these guys," he said. But he had to follow orders, so he broke down his rifle and threw away the parts, then joined the others and waited. But not for long. When the Japanese came, they searched the Americans and Filipinos and stole what they wanted. They killed those holding Japanese souvenirs, then started them on their way.

The Corregidor prisoners weren't taken on the death march with the Bataan Peninsula prisoners, but went directly to fetid, jammed camps. And it was in those camps that the struggle to survive began and didn't let up until victory over three years later.

Farner was a brash kid of 19 thrown into a prison where survival depended on either luck or caution. Farner must have had lots of luck. He quickly learned what brutality was. One day saw a ripe papaya within reach just beyond the barbed wire. He grabbed it, but was seen by a guard. The same day came the reckoning.

"They stood me in the yard and hit me several times across the back with a full swing of a five-foot steel re-bar rod. Each time, it knocked me down. They'd make me get up and do it again. It broke both my arms. Then, they stood me with my head against a wall and had the guards walk by and punch me, knocking my head against the bricks. It fractured my skull. Gosh, that hurt."

To the guards, the spirited Farner served as a handy object lesson to the other prisoners.

Farner and fellow prisoners were transported to Japan on a slow freighter where they were jammed into the dirty hold much of the time. They didn't know it, but American submarines were making a shooting gallery of the China Sea, but the pokey old tub sailed through unscathed.

In Japan, the prisoners were forced into labor details unloading ships. He remembers unloading bags of rice. "They searched us morning and night, but I had found a piece of hacksaw blade, and as we walked through the narrow passages in the hold, I'd reach out and slit the rice bags. The fellows behind me would then grab handfuls of rice. If they'd found that blade, I'da been killed sure."

But when they searched you, how did you conceal it?

"I tied it to my penis."

Farner would sneak into the camp kitchen and liberate rice. "I bribed the guard with cigarettes. But finally, they caught me and put me under guard. All night they kept me awake and beat me. Gosh. In the morning, two American officers were called into a meeting with the Japanese. When they came out, one said, 'They're going to behead you.'

"I told him, 'I won't make it easy. I'll grab a rifle and try to shoot my way out. Either they bring my body back here for you to bury or you'll know I'm up in those mountains.'

"They took me to a room where the guards were gathered. Off to the side, a sergeant was taking practice swings with a heavy sword. The guard I'd bribed was scared and looking at me and shook his head, begging for me not to tell. The officer said I'd been caught stealing and I was gonna have my head cut off. I said, 'You can kill me, but you can't blame me for trying to survive.' I was looking around for a rifle that I could grab while they talked."

It did not escape his notice that the swordsman continued practicing.

"Finally, they said they were just going to beat me again. And they did. They just beat the living hell out of me. But that was fine, just fine."

He spent the remaining slow-moving months in the cold, in sickness and in hunger. But he survived. After the Japanese surrender, the cruelest guards melted into the countryside, but the prisoners didn't molest those remaining; most were older draftees. "They hated being there as much as we did," Farner says, but then pauses. "Well, not really."

Today, Bob Farner can sometimes be seen in north county driving with a large dog and a parrot, both loose in the car. By looks, were the dog human, it would probably sport jailhouse tattoos. That prompts an obvious question.

"No, they're fine together," Farner says. "The dog's well fed and gets lots of affection. He's got no reason to kill. He's not like some people."

The man knows of what he speaks.

(Update: Bob Farner died in 2017.)

Back when monsters were monsters

Bella Lugosi strutting his stuff

Not long ago, I was told of a new "Mummy" movie release starring Tom Cruise. To me, that's a sign of how far culture has fallen. A horror flick featuring an evil Tom Cruise would be like the werewolf guy turning into a Chihuahua.

Who would spill popcorn in fright at Tom Cruise? He has a choir-boy face and is a full head shorter than the average mummy—C'mon, Tom (chuckle, chuckle). You gonna strangle me? Get outta here!

Boris Karloff and Lon Chaney, Jr., now there you had some monsters of respect. Lon was Lou Gehrig to Boris' Babe Ruth. Then, you had your Bela Lugosi. He'd scare his wife just looking over the breakfast toast.

I studied up on this new "Mummy" on Wikipedia, the sloppy researcher's bible. My curiosity did not rise to a $15 ticket.

I read that the movie also has characters named Dr. Jekyll and Mr. Hyde. Excuse me, but weren't those names already taken?

But here's the killer, as we say: the evil mummy is a princess by the name of "Ahmanet," unless I've confused the name with a vodka I saw advertised.

A mummy who's an Egyptian princess? Uh-uh. Cleopatra wrapped in a sheet? Elizabeth Taylor? Ain't happenin'. I can see Liz between sheets, but that was a different movie.

There was a day when horror movies made you proud of Hollywood (or at least the San Fernando Valley). For example, "Attack of the Crab Monsters," which is not to be confused with the Navy training video of the same name.

You wanta mummy? I'll give you one for the ages, which, technically, applies to all mummies, but you know what I'm sayin'.

For the real thing, return with me to the golden age of horror.

Welcome to when I was a kid and you probably weren't even. I'm 10 years old. I got my 50-cent piece in my pocket which I keep patting to make sure it's still there. I'm going to the Egyptian Theater (yes, that was the name) in DeKalb, Illinois.

New Levi's, new Keds on my feet...ohhh, yeah! Like I heard mom say once, I'm steppin' out.

If I can sneak in with the older kids, I'll have enough for popcorn, a box of Dots, and a small Coke. (Jujubes are the in-candy, but I find they stick to the teeth. I stand alone before the Dots display and ignore the stares.)

I'm in the front row, ready for action. I put everything down just right: Popcorn between knees, Dots in hand, Coke on floor between feet. The movie starts. It's "The Mummy's Revenge," or something promising like that.

It's an old movie with thin white lines running vertically through watery-gray film. So what? You don't put the Mummy in Technicolor. He does his best work in black and white.

We begin. It's night, of course, and the hero and his girl are necking in a car out behind the museum where they keep the mummies. Our mummy goes by Karman, or Karma or something like that. The sound system is crackling. There. It's Karnak.

An old guy with a white beard reads the scribbling on the huge box that's holding Karnak. The writing looks like birds and boats, but the guy can read it. He says Karnak did some bad stuff way back when, and it got him put in the box. The old guy opens it anyway.

Karnak gets all irritated because they broke some spell and woke him up after 2,000 years. All that time in a box, he shoulda been grateful. I would be. He never says anything, but what's he got to talk about—baseball?—what with spending all that time all bandaged up and in a box and all.

Karnak is egged on by a weird-talking sneaky guy in a little round hat with a tassel. It's not clear how he figures in.

Anyway, so after Karnak kills the guy who turns him loose, which the guy should've figured might happen anyway, he gets outside, and right away he sees the hero and the blonde necking in this convertible. Oh-oh.

Then he starts—one arm is outstretched, his hand is open, fingers spread, hungry to kill again—I drip my Coke on my new Levi's—He's slowly, slowwwwly dragging a stiff leg along. For sure, he's gonna get them!

My thinking is he wants to kill the guy so he can have the girl all to himself. I don't know why. He can't kiss her with his mouth bandaged over.

Dragging behind him is a loose end of bandage that's coming off his leg, like the tape came loose. Old tape, I guess. His muscles are stiff; you gotta understand, he's been 2,000 years cooped up in a sarcophagus, which I heard someone say is an old name for a big coffin.

At this point, I'm watching the guy in the car make out, and I'm a little curious. Jimmy Boyd told me stuff he heard from Richie Johnson. I asked mom if it was true, and she got mad. Said she was gonna call Richie's mom.

But then I see the mummy getting closer, creeping, dragging that bum leg, reaching out...and the guy and girl are still going at it. They don't know from nothing. They only worry about cops, because cops get upset about stuff like that. Cops you can hear coming.

Oh, no! The mummy is right there! I'm thinking—Look behind you! Start the car! Get out of there, you idiot! C'mon!

I'm all alone in the front row. But I'm not gonna move back 'cause other guys would see me.

Finally, this moron decides to start the car and leave...Oh! No! No! The car won't start! The mummy is almost to the trunk and still they don't look back.

Finally. Thank God! The starter grinds alive and they drive away just in the nick of time, as we used to say. The closest call I've ever seen.

Karnak makes up for it by strangling a lot of people, especially guys in suits and skinny mustaches. At the end, he sinks slowly into quicksand and disappears.

Hah! See how you like 2,000 years down there, Karnak.

But, now...now the real danger begins when I get outside the theater. It's dark, and I'm faced with five blocks to get home. Only a couple of street lights. Made to order for a monster, I'm thinking. I look around—nobody. That's good and that's bad.

I'm not too worried about the Mummy. I'm the third fastest kid in fifth grade, and he's really slow. I won't be caught necking like that guy in the movie. However, there's a full moon, and everybody knows what that means.

I pick up a rock, just in case. I keep looking back. That's how they sneak up on you. The worst part of the run home is past the Catholic church. If I was gonna grab a kid, I'd hide behind one of those statues. I save some speed for that stretch. Good thing I got the new Keds.

Made it!...This time.

San Diego Union-Tribune, September 11, 2017

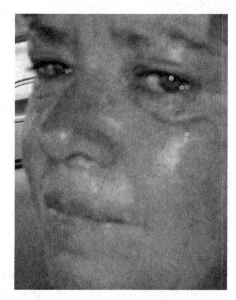

Robin Riddle

Tears can't erase an addicted life

S he is dressed in someone's castoffs and has tears rolling down weather-creased cheeks. She pauses to push back uncombed hair and then returns to drawing circles on the asphalt edge of an Encinitas, Calif. mall parking lot. Open at her side is a box of colored chalk. Her purpose is not clear to me, and perhaps not totally to her. I stop and ask if she's all right.

"No," she says. "My life is only sadness."

I'm on my way to a nearby Subway, anyway, so I change my order to a footlong. I return, and we split the sandwich and talk in the parking lot.

She identifies herself as Robin Riddle. Is that her name? I don't know, but if not, it serves the moment. She is vague about where she's from, and has no idea where she'll be in the future, even tomorrow, although she seems to have become an Encinitas resident.

Robin is an alcoholic, as she makes clear—a homeless alcoholic, the most vulnerable kind. She's also a drug user, when it's available.

She is 53, was born in Florida and has lived in California since age 3. Her rootless life has led her through many doors and onto many streets.

Her home is where she makes it: "I live under any number of bushes that they haven't cut down yet."

I ask what jobs she's had, and she says, "I worked all my life until I dropped out. I've done all things from making pizzas to working in a lot of bars and I have—I probably done some other things, too. I spent some of my life addicted to drugs: white powder drugs, but I'm over that."

How did drugs and alcohol happen to you?

"How did they happen to anyone else? I am old and alcoholic, and I sleep under a bush. That's who I am."

Have you ever worked the streets?

"I have occasionally succumbed to somebody's money for something. Have you?"

I never had any offers.

"I have a couple dollars in my pocket, bro."

She abruptly swings into a drifting stream-of-consciousness, on hyphens] showing a poetic romance with her imagery: "I am assured of my spot on this earth. Without a doubt. Like every plant that spins. Every bit of gas that the air is. You can't have it all."

Robin's mind functions like a machine that's been overworked, or even abused: gears slipping a little, and maybe bearings worn. Then, a switch is flicked and it hums smoothly.

You don't preach to her. She's heard every sermon, ignored every warning.

I ask Robin to describe her day, and she says, "I start my day like everybody else. First thing, I need to go to the restroom at 5:30. The only bathroom that is open is in the (Cardiff State Beach) campground and the fence is still shut. I get up early enough so that I can climb the fence without making a fuss, and then I go to the bathroom and then I brush my hair, my teeth, and I pray. I have a cigarette butt and a drink of vodka."

A cigarette butt? You just pick them up?

"Yeah."

Where do you get the vodka?

"I buy it. I beg on the street for money."

Robin says if she were to go even a day without alcohol she fears the strain on her system would cause a heart attack. "I've been thrown out of eight drug programs. I smoke pot now and it's weaning me off alcoholism. It's very much helping me to get rid of the monkey on my back. I open the cage and I let him go. He comes back now and then, and it's just what it is. Look at everybody running around in their spandex. Everybody is addicted to something. It's a rough road, man. It's really, really hard. It's crushing."

What are your hopes for the future?

"I don't hope."

What do you wish had been?

"I don't."

Robin puts in a full day's work standing in the heat, the sun, the cold and even the rain to beg for money to sustain that monkey. Her begging is born of desperation because without her daily fix of cheap vodka, she knows she likely would lapse into delirium tremens, the dreaded DTs.

"I stand out there with my cardboard sign. Everybody gets to look at me and recognize what my plight is. I get blessed with unconditional love from (givers) who don't even know me."

In the pursuit of vodka money, she's aware of how she's perceived. "I get all kinds of looks. We start at disgusted, and then ignored, and then just plain blank stares…some sympathy, charity."

Being rootless, without resources, she constantly runs the risk of arrest which has happened to her through the years so often she's lost track of the count.

She says that long ago she was a good student. "I graduated on the honor roll early from high school, and I was at college to be an EEG technician…" The thought trails off, lost somewhere in the mist.

Robin has her own version of theology and her place in the world order. "Everything is good. Every day, God takes care of me: Some days chickens, some days feathers. I understand and I feel the love that's generated from God because it's everywhere. Every time you see a leaf blow in the breeze, that's God. You can't stop that. Humans scare me, though. I'm not kidding."

Are you a kind person?

"That's my favorite part about me."

What is your biggest fault?

"My insecurity."

What is that due to?

"My fear."

Of what?

"I'm not sure."

You're an up-front woman, so may I ask if you have a mental illness?

"I like to think I do, but I'm pretty sane."

Robin professes love for her tiny homeless "family" in coastal North County, an affluent outpost with few places of refuge. "I mainly hang out with the guys because girls are mean sometimes."

Do you wish you had a real family and children?

"No. I never wanted them. I'm not responsible like that. I'm a vagabond. I like it like that."

What do you think when you see happy families together?

"I appreciate it."

She knows no happy-highways glamour in her life. "If you (want to) understand what it's like to just completely go without, you need to take my stuff and be there in the dark, under a bush, with a blanket, dirty, hungry, lonely, degraded…

"(If it's raining) you drag your blanket around to an underground parking lot, then here comes a security guard to kick you out, and by that time everything's wet. You just do what you got to do."

On the times that Robin has gotten sick, she says she has gone to the emergency room of the hospital, just across the street from this shopping center, where she is treated with kindness.

She says she has scabies, a mite that burrows into the skin, which she describes as, "A little icky bug. The scabies are horrible man, but they've given me medication over there. It's $72 for a tube of cream, but a nice lady over there just gave it to me."

We may have shared a sandwich, but I'm not one of Robin's trusted family.

"Are you going to tell lies about me?" she asks.

Why would I do that?

"Because you're human."

I give her $5 and say, "I hope this buys some good vodka."

Pleased, she takes the bill, and says, "It won't be good, but it'll be good, if you know what I'm saying."

I do.

✳✳✳

Why do we listen to Robin? Because she has something to say. We can drive by her chalk designs on the pavement and pretend she's not there. But she is. She is there.

San Diego Union-Tribune, September 23, 2013

Trapped in a swirling vortex of pain

B renda Hart's words are as blunt as her life. Answering my phone call, she says, "My life is a negative one. Maybe you want a positive one." Brenda's life story makes me think of the Slough of Despond in "The Pilgrim's Progress," except that John Bunyan's spiritual ditch was for sin and guilt. Brenda's despair is not of her doing, but of an age-old malady that modern medicine cannot cure.

Brenda is a 44-year-old single woman. She's kind of frumpy, but that's the least of her worries. Brenda is afflicted with bipolar disorder and is schizoaffective. That's

Brenda Hart

about the mental illness equivalent of cancer and pneumonia combined. You can tell by looking at her that something's not quite right.

In common terms, she occasionally sees things that aren't there, and sometimes has trouble making her thoughts travel in a straight line. Her moods can go from elation to black depression like a shutter click. In the brain of the afflicted, mental illness is a pied piper leading into a room of distorted mirrors.

Brenda is important because there are so many Brendas, of both sexes, and we don't know them. They often don't know themselves.

Her disease started quite early, and perhaps was speeded along by a screwed-up childhood. "My relationship with my parents was really bad. There are certain things that happened to me as a child that were tragic, and I think had something to do with my mental illness." She is completely alienated from her parents. "I wouldn't cry if they died."

Brenda dropped out of high school and then got married at 21—bad idea—and had three children before divorcing her husband. One child she gave up for adoption; the other two she has no contact with, but she knows their names and ages: Daniel Allen, 24 or 25, and Yahshua, who is 22 or 23. ("That's Jesus in Hebrew," she adds helpfully.)

"I would like to see them again, but I don't know how to do it. I can't afford to go to Spokane, and I couldn't afford to stay in a motel," she says in a flat monotone, probably a benign side effect of one of the drugs she is on, as prescribed by her psychiatrist.

She now lives in a board and care facility in San Diego's Golden Hill. She shares a bedroom with another woman in the older, large house that seems quiet and clean. Her rent is paid by her Social Security disability (SSI) benefits. It's a sad place to visit because all the others who live there are also mentally ill. However, residents are free to come and go, and activities are planned to lighten their lives: movies, shopping trips to Walmart, an outing to the fair. Brenda sometimes goes out for a meal by herself at McDonald's.

Several residents are sitting on the porch as I arrive, and everyone smiles and says hello. Others are in the parlor sitting and watching TV, but not with much engagement. Some seem a bit vacant, but all are friendly, as they almost always are. As a group, the mentally ill under treatment are about as dangerous as a nun on a well-lit street.

It's hard to imagine this place being a refuge; you and I would shudder at the prospect of having no place to go but here. However, for Brenda and the others, this is a peaceful haven.

After picking her up for lunch, I invited her to choose any place, thinking it's probably been a while since she's been to a white-tablecloth restaurant. Her choice was a taco stand.

She is deeply curious about why she is the way she is, in the same way a cancer patient reads up on oncology. She attends chapter meetings of the National Alliance on Mental Illness because, she says, "It's a good place for people like me to learn stuff about getting better."

For most of the past 12 years—she's not sure how many—Brenda lived on the streets of San Diego, frequently drunk, sometimes high, and very often out of her mind. She was one of the mentally ill homeless who are part reality and part myth in every large city in America. Brenda was a person you drive past without noticing, and, depressingly, she might be once again. The danger is always there.

In 2000 or 2001, Brenda isn't sure which, she took some SSI funds and left her hometown of Spokane for San Diego, where the sun did shine and there was no snow.

"When I got to San Diego, I was homeless right off the bus. I panicked because I didn't have all my medications. I was like, 'What am I going to do?' I didn't know where to go to get something to eat or where to get help. So I was stuck."

She woke up in a hospital psych ward. "I guess the cops picked me up." Thus began a decade-long series of round-trips between streets and hospitals. Once back on the street, she would neglect the medications given her, which would lead to episodes of mental breakdown, again followed by hospitalization, then back to the streets. She lost track of her SSI benefits. She lived wherever she found herself at the moment.

Brenda's chronology often doesn't square. Years and thoughts trip over each other. On being homeless, she says, "It was off and on, sometimes it was seven years, and one time it was—I don't know if it was really seven years. It might have been another year. I was just thinking it was that long, you know, cause it, I mean, I was not taking my meds, and I'd get delusional and think things that are different, and, uh, I think it was another year, and sometimes it would be six months."

The public hears about homeless people discarding medications and wonders why, often with exasperation. Brenda explains it's not always a wanton act. Many drugs used for the mentally ill have severe side effects that require monitoring. However, since hospitals can't keep people against their will, these patients may end up coping on their own with the drugs' sometimes nasty side effects. You might as well ask them to explain the Higgs boson particle as to manage their own treatment.

"When I was homeless, the cops would pick me up and take me to the hospital, or sometimes to jail, because I'd be drunk in public and yelling and screaming and talking to myself. I was out of it without my meds, because I'd just throw them away because of the way they made me feel. Geodon made my nose bleed, Paxil made me feel like climbing the walls. And others were as bad. So when I was put in a different hospital, I'd get put on new drugs."

And the cycle would repeat itself: delusions and hallucinations. "This one time I went into Macy's, and, uh, I took some stuff thinking my dad had bought it for me, and then I got in trouble. I was holding the stuff in my hands and walking out the door. I don't remember what all it was. Then, I got arrested. I told the police I was sorry. I don't know if they took me to jail. I don't remember. They probably did."

Hallucinations terrified Brenda. "I would hear my name being called, and I'd be looking for the person who called my name, and there'd be nobody there. And I would see scary black silhouettes that were like shadows of people. I'd see something that looked like a cat and I don't think it was really there."

Worse, she saw evil ghosts. "One time, I saw the Grim Reaper." Terrifying.

Living on the street was a lonely time for Brenda, even when surrounded by crowds of people during the day and fellow dwellers at night. "(Street people) were only my friends if I had something to drink. If I didn't, they weren't around. I just wanted to be by myself. If someone offered something, yeah, I would take it. But if nobody offered, I'd just drink by myself."

To Brenda, drinking meant a vile concoction I had never heard of called Four Loko. Brenda describes it as 12 percent malt liquor with a super injection of caffeine in a fruit flavor. Ugh. But its reputation didn't lie. It did the promised job.

"Most times I wouldn't sleep because I was drinking Four Lokos. It's guaranteed to keep you both drunk and energized at the same time. The first time I ever had one, I ended up lying on my back, and when I came to, the rain was falling on me."

She would also smoke weed on the occasions when another homeless person would share with her.

"One time, when I was talking to myself and screaming profanities. This one guy, he thought I was talking to him. He came up to me like he was going to beat me up. I was really scared. I was telling him over and over again, 'I wasn't talking to you. I wasn't talking to you.'"

A typical day on the streets would be spent going through garbage cans for food or to find aluminum cans for a little spending money. "I'd find chicken or sandwiches, some partially eaten. Sometimes people would come up and give me some food." She would also go to downtown churches or charity facilities for food.

Every couple of weeks or so, she would go to grocery store restrooms to clean up, wash her clothes and put on her clean set. There, she wouldn't be bothered. She avoided gas station restrooms because "people would be banging on the door.

"I didn't have boyfriends when I was homeless; just didn't want to." She was never raped, a common danger on the streets. She also wasn't tempted to turn to prostitution. "No, I wouldn't do that. I'd rather look for cans and stuff."

Brenda declares herself a believing Christian, but says religion was of little benefit to her when she was on the streets.

She has been stabilized for over a year, first in the Alpine Special Treatment Center, a lockdown facility that she voluntarily entered. She then became stable enough to move to her present board and care, after her SSI situation was untangled. She is currently on three medications, the names of which she painstakingly printed out on lined paper: Depakote, Risperdal and Lamictal. These drugs are her friends, but only so long as she is faithful to them. Thus far, she has stayed with the regimen.

She dreams of becoming a graphic designer because she likes to draw, but she's had no experience with computers and is uncertain how one goes about such a thing. Yet she has signed up for two classes at San Diego City College—in general ed and beginning computers.

Brenda is trying. She never quit trying.

She'd appreciate having a companion, a fella with whom she could share things, but she's not hungry for that. She'd just like it.

I don't think Brenda knows any fulfillment beyond momentary satisfaction. She is never out of danger from herself. She is aware that, at any time, some insult or stress could set her off and she might dump her meds, return to the streets and again sleep on concrete and drink Four Lokos. It would not be what she wants, but in her brain, compulsion can beat down choice like an angry bully.

Brenda is friendly with a crinkly-face laugh. She is open and trusting. You would like her, especially knowing her burdens. Imagine, if you will, having no contact with the three children you birthed, being estranged from your parents and not even trusting them, having no one to whom you can turn for love, and every moment knowing that a shade can drop on reality.

Brenda Hart is trapped in a vortex of swirling winds that pry at her finger-hold on reality and threaten to again spin her life out of control. Her struggle has no end.

And yet, she smiles.

San Diego Union-Tribune, August 12, 2012

Woman thought of kids she helped as she neared her end

Janet Vaughn sits half-inclined on her bed and thinks of a tomorrow. But hers will not be the tomorrow the rest of us envision. Her mind is on a coming-soon tomorrow that will see her struggle for one more breath, but then find that there are no more. On that tomorrow, Janet Vaughn will die.

Janet is in home hospice, which means she officially is waiting for the end, usually within six months. Janet is on her eighth month. Hospice is a limbo between the end of hope and the end. According

Janet Vaughn

to Janet, it's actually a place of some relief because all the guess-work is done. Hospice is the last word.

Janet is a 69-year-old single mother who lives in a pleasant Oceanside, Calif. home with roses out front that once were lovingly kept. Living with her and helping with her care is her adult daughter, April, and a yorkie named Pickles.

She was diagnosed 3 1/2 years ago with congestive heart failure. Until last year, she regularly dragged herself to the doctor only to hear the same words that marked her descent, step by gasping, hurting step. Finally, she was told there would be no recovery. Only time remained. Time as a fading wisp.

* * *

Now, knowing the future, but with nothing to do but wait for it, she has time to think, to leaf through the pages of receding years. She keeps coming back to the memory of taking into her home and caring for 105 sick children, mainly drug babies, as a foster parent for Orange County Social Services. They were infants born into a world that didn't welcome them. She knows the number, she says, because each one was important to her.

Her body carries a great amount of water that it cannot process. That's called edema, a matter-of-fact clinical term that doesn't describe the laborious shifting in bed and the slow dragging across the floor to the bathroom that it causes. She is bed-bound and can only rarely struggle to her family room recliner. She can't see the sun or watch the rain from her bedroom.

Even so, Janet doesn't see the glass as only half full: it's full to the brim. "Finally, I don't have to get up, get dressed and struggle to the doctor's," she says. "The hospice caretakers come to me. I see the nurse once a week, and the woman who changes the sheets and gets my medicines and stuff also comes once a week. It's now just waiting."

Just waiting. She says that as other people might say they're "just waiting" for American Idol to start.

She is on about 25 different medications, including all the morphine she can tolerate and oxygen that's ramped up to the max. But even with all that, Janet remains cheerful. "What's the point of feeling sorry for myself?" she asks. "I know what's going to happen, and I have my faith to sustain me. It's a beautiful life." On the wall nearby is a framed portrait of Christ. It is not there as décor. She does not have a death wish, but a wish to die well.

* * *

To Janet, the dying process is a walk that she knows will soon end, but she will take each step to prove that on her last day she will be upbeat and squared-away with her reality. "People seem to think that when you're dying you're too depressed to talk about it. Why shouldn't you? People like to talk about their lives. Well, this is my life—still."

Okay, one thinks, but that's right now, this pleasant afternoon. How about those wee, small hours of the morning that the ballad warns us of? Does she not wake in the early dawn's grayness, all alone, stare at the ceiling and ask the eternal rhetorical questions: Why me? Why now?

"Sure, I get down, get depressed. My mind feels the pain, and the thoughts that I will no longer see my children. I wonder how my grandchildren will develop. I'll never drive along the beach again. But I don't let that take control of me." She pauses, starts to say something, then doesn't.

Her thoughts come back to the children. Always the children. She sees their faces, unchanged for all the years. That she held them, fed them, and diapered them is an affirmation of the belief she wants to leave behind: "I tried hard to serve other people. If you do that, it will make you feel glad to be alive."

She wants to be remembered for her cheerfulness. That's a modest-sounding goal until one thinks about how tough it is for the rest of us to stay cheerful for a whole day. For those who will remember her, it's what she hopes they occasionally mention.

Sounds like the idyllic life. But no, she objects. "I had all the troubles of an ordinary person; worse than some, not as bad as others: Marriage problems, money problems, child-raising problems, and certainly health problems. I'm pretty much just like you and everyone else. But so what? This is not the time for a pity party."

* * *

Her son is flying in from Texas this day. She has a chocolate cake for him that says, "Love you, Bri." It might be a final reunion. Janet will not allow it to be a sad one.

On a later day, Janet leans back on her pillows and points to a row of pills on the nightstand. "Please hand me my nitroglycerin pills," she asks, pointing toward the table, and says with a merry laugh. "Over there. Right next to the birth control pills."

She turns serious. "The nurse was just here and said my lungs are unchanged, but my heart is getting weaker. My memory is worse and I have a bad pain in my arm. All I can do is hobble to the bathroom."

She says she'd like another chocolate cake, and that she wouldn't hesitate to eat it. "I won't worry about my waistline." She laughs wanly, determined not to shrink from the approaching shadow.

As days slip into weeks, her disease presses down with strength-sapping pressure. Willpower drains with fatigue. Gradually, resistance is lowered, and what lies ahead is less feared. It will work its will.

"I'm dying. I feel it, and I know it. And I'm ready."

Soon, the ambulance will come and back into the driveway, and then will drive quietly away with no need to hurry. Janet's house will be sold. Her daughter will move away, taking Pickles on his leash. The neighbors will meet the newcomers and then forget the woman who used to live there. But those to whom she spoke of her values, they will remember her. For awhile. Then Janet will become one with the spirit of others who also once lived and tried.

(Update: Janet Vaughn died soon after this story ran.)

San Diego Union-Tribune, April 29, 2012

Hope is what this mother has left

Lynn Evans comes down the stairs just as her daughter, Kim, is about to leave. Kim is dressed casually in olive shorts and a plaid top, neatly, as always. She has her carry-on-size suitcase in hand, and one of her two laptops. She's headed for the front door.

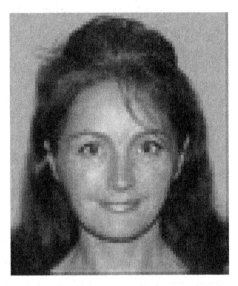

Kim Evans

Kim is a 41-year-old writer who has lived in her mother's Encinitas, California townhouse for a year. Earlier that morning, they engaged in a strong argument, but Lynn has no idea Kim intends to leave.

"I'm terribly sorry, mother," Kim says, referring to their disagreement. Then she moves toward the door, and says, "I'll be back." She hesitates, and adds, "soon," and then the door closes behind her.

* * *

That was late morning April 30, 2013, and "soon" never happened. Kimberly Jo Evans has not been heard from since.

Her disappearance has been complete, as though she never existed. It's left behind only a single word—

Missing.

It's a word that sits heavy, alternatively offering dread, then hope, then dread again, as it flashes like a strobe in the mind of Kim's mother.

With the abuse of passing time, dread grows like mold and hope fades from the glare of reality. Lynn can only stare out her daughter's bedroom window, waiting. For 15 months, waiting.

Lynn sees her daughter walk out the door for the thousandth time, and recycles the taunting possibilities for which there are no answers, and might never be.

* * *

It never starts out that way. Kim was a typical kid with carloads of friends all through La Jolla High School and was often a leader in the types of things teenage girls do.

She graduated from Cal Poly San Luis Obispo and spent productive years in public relations and then as a writer of books and blogs on diet and natural living with some success. Though never married, she's had romantic relationships, but shied away from men who might be abusive or not respectful of her standards of healthful living, which were scrupulous.

In the year Kim lived with her mother, she formed no friendships. She had a strained relationship with her step-father and almost no contact with her birth father.

* * *

The incident that led to Kim's walking out happened when her mother awoke on that same day and realized Kim had "cleaned" Lynn's grandmother's piano, but with a mixture of garlic juice and baking soda.

"It was all streaked with white and the wax had turned color. The keys would push down but not come up, so she'd gotten it in between the keys," Lynn says.

Lynn was shocked and upset when she saw the damage to the piano, and told Kim she would have to either take the medicine prescribed to settle her down, or leave the house.

As normally happens in mother-daughter quarrels, things quieted down. However, Lynn continued to insist that the medicine be taken which Kim did not believe in.

* * *

Later, after Kim had not returned, Lynn inventoried what she had taken with her: about $400 cash, her passport and one of her two laptops. She owned neither credit cards nor a cell phone. And—most worrisome—to this day Kim has not touched her checking account which still holds almost $1,000.

Because Kim had left home for short periods from time to time, Lynn waited two weeks then contacted the sheriff's department, and Kim was listed as a missing person. She was reminded by a deputy that adults have the right to leave and to be left alone, and even to disappear.

As Kim's absence grew longer, the case was assigned to the homicide unit as a matter of routine. The State Department put a watch on her passport; Social Security reported that her number had not been used; even Interpol put her on a watch list. The FBI examined her other computer and found nothing suspicious, and nothing that indicated a destination or even a desire to leave home. Police phone searches also revealed nothing.

As of February of this year, if she uses her passport, it will be reported to the sheriff's department. The problem is, in the intervening nine or so months since the disappearance, she could have gone anywhere.

* * *

Lynn says she is satisfied with law enforcement efforts, but has also used two private investigators; all efforts have been fruitless.

She even hired a psychic. "I was desperate; what can I tell you?" she says with a shrug in her voice.

She has contacted the American consulate in Tijuana and they have checked hospitals, prisons and morgues, with no results. San Diego police maintain a liaison in Tijuana, and she hopes they are also watching for Kim, but Mexican police by reputation are not burdened with an abundance of competence.

* * *

Lynn describes her daughter as being of a supple and inquisitive intellect with creativity bursting out all over—a painter in oils, a photographer, a clear writer with style, and even an open-water diver.

She says her daughter is a world traveler: Europe, Thailand and throughout the Americas. She also credits Kim with survival skills. "Once when she was in South America and found herself short of money, she went panning for gold."

Her mother says Kim neither drinks nor does drugs and is very particular about her diet which is heavy on vegetables and nuts.

However, a nagging question won't go away: Is Kim mentally ill?

Despite spells of aberrant behavior, her mother refuses to believe it. "I absolutely don't think so. I'm not a doctor, but (her behavior) doesn't have the signs I've read about."

She says she has accompanied Kim to three psychiatrists and none would commit to a diagnosis of mental illness. "They couldn't quite figure Kim out, either.

"They thought she was uncooperative and didn't want to follow traditional medicine, which is true. She doesn't believe in going to doctors. She believes in natural healing and natural herbs and that kind of thing. (All three doctors) would ask me what I thought. I just didn't know."

Lynn tells of an experience Kim had related to her that stemmed from a visit to Ecuador three years ago. In a native semi-religious ceremony, Kim ingested some sort of cactus derivative which she believed left her possessed by a demon, and which takes over her actions from time to time. She didn't tell Lynn if the demon is figurative or literal.

Lynn has maintained contact with the large American colony in Ecuador and does not think Kim is there.

Lynn says the sheriff's detective assigned to Kim's case, Dave Hillen, gently told her she might never see her daughter again.

The detective spoke the truth that many families push out of their minds, which is that Lynn might *not* ever see Kim again. That could, of course, mean she would be unable to return, or would chose not to. The detective was also trying to instill some balance in Lynn's thinking for the long haul. Unrealistic hope is a shooting star that will soon leave the observer blinking in the darkness.

Hillen refused to comment on the case.

I sought the opinion of two missing-person and homicide professionals to talk in generalities about worst-case possibilities. They are anonymous because of uneasiness at commenting on a colleague's case.

They both give reasons for guarded optimism that Kim is alive.

Although all of Southern California, plus Mexico, is proximate to ocean and desert, those aren't necessarily practical in disposing of a body.

One expert pointed out that to dispose of a body at sea requires a good-sized boat, and then getting the heavy, awkward weight of a body aboard unseen; digging a grave in the back country would be hard work, can be observed by hikers, and requires the risk of driving many miles with a body in the car. A shallow grave can be dug up by animals.

The heart of the experts' optimism is that if a predator abducts and kills a woman with whom he has no known ties, he is usually in haste to abandon the body in a convenient, semi-hidden place which is often soon discovered.

Lynn says Kim has a keen antenna about being near suspicious or weird men and would not be gullible or compliant when faced with danger.

She also says that Kim would never feel safe or be comfortable in areas where homeless people congregate, and would certainly stand out.

Kim would not be a candidate for ransom or theft. And as a savvy, cautious middle-aged woman, would not be as vulnerable a sexual target as a naïve or incautious girl.

A predator seeks success, not challenge. The wolf does not attack a wolverine; it goes after a deer.

For all these reasons, both experts are unwilling to assume she's no longer alive. Both, however, find the untapped bank account troubling.

These thoughts are not happy talk, of course, but they are straws to grasp when there is little else to hold on to.

The months on Lynn's calendar and marked off by tears as she prays for the return of her talented daughter of spontaneous spirit.

"Whenever Kim would need help, she would always contact me. That she hasn't, worries me. I am totally convinced that she had every intention of coming back in a matter of days."

Lynn knows there's a chance Kim might still be in San Diego, and if that is true, she hopes that her mother's plea will be heard and cause her daughter to come home. "I want to tell her how much I love, value her and miss her."

When a child is out in the cold, a mother will never stop looking and never stop hoping.

The reason hope is so durable is that it sometimes comes true.

(Update: Kim Evans is still missing.)

San Diego Union-Tribune, August 4, 2014

Saved from the Holocaust by a determined mother

This is a small story from the time the world collapsed. However, it would not be a story at all but for the stubbornness of a smart woman who said: I will not allow this family to die.

* * *

Jack Keisman

The 12-year-old boy was shaken awake by his father. "You don't have to go to school today, Jack." The boy blinked the sleep out of his eyes. His quizzical look asked why. "The Germans invaded Belgium today."

The date was May 10, 1940. The place was 43 Montenegro St., Brussels, Belgium.

Not a good date nor a good place for young Isaac "Jack" Keisman to start his day. It was the beginning of a not-very-good year for the young Jew and his family.

Keisman, now an 85-year-old retired Chicago manufacturer, can look back 73 years on those events with the clarity of a picture album, but one with some pages best not lingered on.

What was facing young Jack, his family, and all of Europe, was the beginning of full-scale hostilities.

* * *

The British army had landed on the continent months earlier, in September 1939, to join with the French and Belgian armies to resist the expected German offensive. But when it happened, it took the Wermacht less than a month to overrun France, the Netherlands and Belgium, forcing Allied armies to the shores of the English Channel. Swept along were a road-clogging stream of refugees who recalled the German cruelty of World War I only 22 years previous.

The human surge ended at the French coastal town of Dunkerque, or Dunkirk, almost 100 miles northwest of Brussels, and at ocean-front towns for miles in both directions. Over the following two weeks, about 1,000 ships and boats from England would rescue over 300,000 soldiers. But until that happened, desperation reigned.

The Keisman family, parents and two young sons, had joined the exodus, and ended up in Coxyde, about 15 miles from Dunkirk. A half-mile in front of the empty home the family occupied were thousands of British Tommies trapped on the beach, hoping for rescue from the sea, but fearful of the German juggernaut that approached from the land.

"It was a big adventure for me," Keisman says. "I went down and wandered among the soldiers on the beach. They were trapped. I saw guys just a half-dozen years older than I. Some were dumping heavy equipment they figured they'd never need again. Some were sitting around in the sand playing cards or writing letters. Everyone was smoking cigarettes and most were pretty quiet. No one was laughing or joking. Nothing was funny. A lot just stared out to sea, hoping for ships that might or might not show up.

"They knew the Germans had whipped them. They figured they were coming and couldn't be stopped. And from the way they kept looking inland, figured they might be just over one of the nearby hills. The lines to the latrine were long. I didn't realize it at the time, but most probably figured they'd be taken prisoner or killed within days."

* * *

Excited by his new adventure, young Keisman was unaware that as events unfolded, death would be more likely for him than for most of these soldiers.

Reality intruded on the scene when Keisman watched a German fighter swoop down and strafe his six-year-old brother playing in the street. To this day, he can hear the sewing-machine sound of the guns and the roar of the plane's engine. "I watched the bullets hit and kick up dust just in front of him and just behind. He came within a few feet of dying, but he just kept on playing."

On June 3, the day the last of the British were sea-lifted out, the artillery barrage was especially strong. He can recall the whistle of the shells arching over the town to explode on the beach.

The next morning the British were gone, and the day dawned quiet. Eerily quiet, considering. Then came the muffled thud of boots as lines of German infantry marched into town.

There was nowhere to go except back to Brussels where they arrived on the twenty-first day since they fled.

"No one knew what would happen, but everyone was worried," he says. "However, in the Jewish district, there was straight-up panic. It was no secret what the Germans had been doing to the Jews—the jailings, the beatings, the confiscations, and all the rest. Hitler hated Jews. We knew that. We didn't know at the time, however, just how much he hated us."

The Keismans lived in an upscale Gentile area where they operated a prosperous leather-clothing company. The concerns in that neighborhood were more muted, but Fannie, his mother, 37, wasn't fooled. In 1938, she had deposited $16,000 (about $250,000 today) in a New York bank, believing that proof of affluence would make obtaining U.S. visas easier. It did. She got them.

"My dad was an optimistic salesman-type. He believed he could talk himself into or out of anything, and usually he could. To him, business was good, so why leave? Mom, though, had a sharp eye for what was going on. She got it."

* * *

Life returned to normal except the Germans took over public buildings and mounted signs that proclaimed officious tongue-twisters like "kommandantur" in all-caps. Keisman says the Germans went on a PR campaign to show what nice guys they were. But despite the glad-handing, he recalls everything they said seemed to be shouted, even when talking to each other.

Frequent companions were Keisman's two cousins, Sarah, 10, and Leidish, 20. Today, he remembers them by showing their pictures in the Holocaust website, Yad Vashen, where their photos are frozen in time as victims of a Nazi death camp. They, their parents, and other Keisman relatives now are found only in a digital file, their dreams unfulfilled, their careers unrealized, their children unborn.

Keisman said the mood in the city was resignation. "They weren't mean to us; they changed a few things, but they didn't bother anybody at that time. We hated them because, you know, they were the boche. But collaborators were all over the place. You could see it all around you. People look for easy ways to make money, to have power. My dad could be called one; he did business with them." Keisman's father made a lot of money selling full-length, green-dyed leather coats to German officers, the type you can see in war movies.

His mother's intuition was raging. Things seemed pretty normal, but Fannie Keisman knew better. She told Joseph that it was time to go. He protested that times were good, and young Jack heard the arguing. Finally, with her American visas in hand, she said, I'm taking the boys and you can come if you wish. That settled it.

Keisman says he was in downtown Brussels when he saw a line of people stretching around the corner. Curious, he walked up and learned they were Jews registering to be given the yellow cloth in the shape of the Star of David to sew onto their coats. One man was dressed in the cassock of a Catholic priest, obviously one with Jewish "blood." It was supposed to be a badge of shame for being Jews.

* * *

Two days later, in December, the family departed Belgium wearing no yellow stars.

The Germans gladly gave them exit visas through France, and the Spanish allowed them to transit to the Portuguese border where the plan was to board a ship in Lisbon for New York. The only things young Keisman knew about the U.S. was everyone had an automobile, Roosevelt, and the Statue of Liberty.

All went well until a Portuguese border guard noticed their American visas had expired. Keisman remembers his mother shrieking and crying when they were denied entry into Portugal. She knew their lives were at stake.

He speculates his mother must have known the visas had expired; she was too smart not to, but must have decided to gamble that harried border guards would carelessly overlook it, but by then they'd have a refuge in neutral Portugal. Desperation has its own logic.

No choice remained but to return to France. They left the train at the border town of Hendaye where they lived in a boarding house for three months, sharing a dinner table with German officers who generally ignored them.

That early in the war, before things started to turn against the Axis, and Europe was still a Nazi fortress, life was at least a semblance of normal in France. There were food shortages, arrests were sudden but not very common, and if a German gave an order, people were quick to obey, but they found it manageable.

One day, a knock on the boarding house door gave entry to two German soldiers who told his parents to come with them. The dreaded arrest. Keisman, then 13, assumed he would never see his parents again. In fact, just before leaving, his father reminded him of the diamonds sewn into the lining of a briefcase. He watched them grow small walking down the cobblestones with a soldier on either side.

But to his surprise, and probably theirs, his parents were released. He was never told why, and assumes his parents didn't know either.

Keisman witnessed a telling breach in his father's upbeat veneer when he broke down in tears at being rebuffed for new visas at the nearby American consulate in Bordeaux. Consequently, his parents decided to move to Paris and plead at the American embassy.

When they first saw the embassy, their hearts sank at the lines circling the building like the coils of a rope. Inundated by refugees who, like his mother, had finally figured out that only persecution lay behind them, embassy officials had given out numbers to the desperate petitioners. Keisman saw that the numbers were in the hundreds.

The next day, his father disappeared, and then returned to show them the number he had obtained for the next day: one. "How?" young Jack asked. "It cost more than a can of chicken soup," Joseph said with a smile.

* * *

While the family waited in Paris for the promised visas to be approved, they spent much of their time just trying to eat regularly. Meals often consisted of rutabagas and leathery, stringy meat from unknown animal sources. Again, Joseph worked his charm. Once, he told a shopkeeper he was an opera singer and needed onions to maintain his voice. He got them.

As the Jew-hating ratcheted up in the Third Reich, the pressure was felt in Paris. The refugees had little to do except wait and hang out, often together. Keisman remembers one Jew who wore his Iron Cross won in the first war and was frequently saluted by German soldiers who walked past. The proud ex-soldier told them Hitler would have been good for Germany, except, "Why did he have to persecute the Jews?"

Young Jack hooked up with a street-wise refugee of his own age from Germany named Leon Schmaltz who showed him the naughtiness of Paris. Leon took him to a burlesque house. That was the moment, he says, that he discovered there was more to manhood than a bar mitzvah. With eyes fastened on the stage, the all-knowing Leon cautioned him, "They don't have anything like this in America."

With new visas gripped tightly, the family again made the trip through Spain, and this time were admitted to Portugal and on to Lisbon.

On May 10, 1941, one year to the day of the invasion of Belgium, Jack Keisman and his family embarked for America to see the Statue of Liberty on one of the last refugee ships to leave Europe. It was a good day to be alive.

Today, as an old man looking back over a long and successful life, Keisman reminds us that in 1940, Europe, not the U.S., was the center of the world. And he was in the middle as it teetered on the fulcrum of history. He further knows that, were it not for a mother who refused to let her family be Nazi victims, he would exist today only as a teenage image on the Holocaust website.

(Update: Jack Keisman died in 2014.)

San Diego Union-Tribune, February 18, 2013

He fights for free speech in an unlikely place

Naweed Tahmas

When Socrates stood before the judges to defend his right to free speech, he said, "If you turn me free on the condition that I no longer speak my mind...I shall say to you, 'Men of Athens, I shall obey the gods, rather than you.'"

Found guilty, he was compelled to drink poison.

Today, 2,416 years later, Socrates might survey the suppression of free speech on college campuses, throw up his hands in disgust, and say, "For this I drank hemlock?"

In college, I loved the rhetorical sparring between ideologies, left, right, far out and far in. It taught me that democracy is not built on agreement alone, but even more so on disagreement, and how sides come together—by respect and compromise.

In journalism, I realized you could make a living with those beliefs. Free money. So, do I believe in free speech? You might as well ask an engineer if she believes in math. And nonpartisan reporting? It's the Golden Rule. And reporters who think they know better than readers? Straight to hell.

Personally, I'm a traditional liberal. That means everyone has a reason to disagree with me, and I want to make sure they have the chance.

I don't care what you are. If you have views different from mine, you're important to me because I need you for balance. If everyone believed as I do, and with no conflicting ideas barring our way, we would push each other to disastrous extremes, because there would be no one to protect us from ourselves.

On the other hand, maybe I should have listened to mom who said I should consider becoming a humanities professor. At least then I could be protected from unwelcome ideas.

* * *

Naweed Tahmas is the attentive guy in the front row of class whose arm shoots up first with the answer. He thinks with a bean-counter exactitude that's earned him an A-minus GPA. (Said with respect by one whose beans often conduct themselves mischievously.)

He's quiet and precise; the only political science major I can recall who doesn't pronounce it "poly sci."

He's an articulate, handsome guy of 21 who intends to be a lawyer. If I had a daughter of 20, I would have brought her along to the interview.

Do I sound impressed?...Yeah, guess I do.

Naweed grew up in Oceanside, Calif., the son of middle class white-collar immigrants. He's was a community college product before transferring to Berkeley. I first assumed he was of Indian descent (which many do, he says), but he's a first-generation Persian of Christian persuasion with ancestors from Tajikistan and Iran.

Persian is an ethnicity, he says, Iranian is a nationality. The distinction is important to him or he wouldn't have mentioned it.

(Thanks for offering the information, Naweed, but let me lay that burden down and just call you an American.)

Naweed is vice president of the Berkeley College Republicans, a beleaguered club of a few dozen students, one of whom is his girlfriend. (Maybe students who think alike...uh, study together.)

He is also a Trump supporter and, frankly, our president can cause me more anguish than a stubbed toe. However, I couldn't care less about Naweed's politics. This is about his voice, not his vote.

Naweed chose to be a political contrarian on one of the most leftist campuses in the country. They don't need First Amendment protection, he does. His experience is a reminder that freedom of speech is not about protecting the words that others want to hear, but the words they don't want to hear.

On Feb. 1, 2017, Naweed found himself a point man in the battle for free speech that has invaded college campuses nation-wide like hungry locusts.

It is ironic that the nastiest attack (thus far) was at U.C. Berkeley, which was given the nickname "Berserkly" for its free-speech conflicts of the '60s and '70s. At that time, it was thought free speech had won, but recent events remind us that skirmishes don't decide a war.

* * *

Milo Yiannopoulos is a gay, conservative provocateur. He was scheduled to speak on the Berkeley campus on Feb. 1. Yiannopoulos relishes offending antagonists by saying outrageous things. Naturally, that horrifies many students and can even send some fleeing to "safe spaces."

(You young dopes, don't you realize that's what he's trying to do? That's his shtick. It's a wild form of argumentation, but argumentation it is, ask any comedian.)

A footnote: "safe spaces" and "trigger warnings" are safeguards concocted to "protect" students from ideas that might otherwise bruise their sensibilities and psyches; you know, those same ideas they had gone to school to learn about, and which they will have to deal with in the real world they will shortly be cast into—or onto.

When the Yiannopoulos event was due to start, leftist rioters attacked event supporters, destroyed state property, and started fires to burn offending banners.

Police ringed the "demonstration" and did virtually nothing, as the press widely reported. Naweed and his group had to take refuge behind locked doors.

Naweed says police were under orders to "stand down" as the vandals rioted and threatened with impunity. Millions of TV viewers saw the cops doing just that as they watched the hoodlums cavort.

I asked a university PR staffer for a reply to charges that the police were prevented from enforcing the law by higher-ups.

The PR guy deflected the question and said police don't like to aggressively act unless they have a 3 to 1 cop-power edge on rioters. They were mainly interested in protecting lives, not property.

Can't they multitask? They had a loudspeaker, guns, clubs, tear gas, tasers, and who knows what else. Maybe a tank around the corner. How big an edge do they need?

A few weeks later, a speech on campus had been scheduled for conservative Ann Coulter. The gravest threat of needle-tongue Coulter is that she might leave her audience thrashing on the floor in fits of irritation. However, her appearance was cancelled due to barriers put on her appearance by the university, Naweed says.

My PR interview went nowhere. Think political spinners on TV, and you'll understand why clumps of my hair littered the ground. In summary, the spokesman said the university welcomes all conservative speakers, treats the students who invite them fairly, and...let's leave it at that.

The college Republicans have filed a federal civil rights lawsuit claiming the university violated students' rights to free speech. As policy, U.C. Berkeley will not comment on a pending lawsuit.

When I think of thugs attacking people because they don't believe the right things, I think that's probably what Robespierre did before he discovered the efficiency of shutting mouths by chopping heads.

* * *

Naweed related several incidents of members of his group being harassed on campus. However, the bigger problem for all students, and the gravest implication for American education, is in the classroom where he says conservative students are treated like aliens—from Mars, not Mexico.

Do you feel free to speak up in class?

"What I've noticed when I speak up is that a bad relationship with the professor grows—" He pauses. "Let me reword that. I want to say this in a diplomatic way."

It's diplomatic enough for me.

"Professors tend to not like me after I speak up in class or I challenge their views. I think my arguments irritate them, and they take it very personally.

"One time, there was a professor that initially liked me at the beginning of the semester; told me that I'm the exact student she'd been looking for. (However,) I disagreed with her one time, and after class she sat down next to me and said, 'Naweed, I'm very disappointed in you.' All because I dared challenge her views.

"The topic (I challenged) had to do with this idea of victim-hood for minorities. I gave her examples of my family's story, and how they were able to become successful. But she didn't look fondly on that."

In a political theory class, he says another professor issued a "trigger warning" for sensitive students about a passage he was about to read from Thomas Hobbes' "Leviathan."

But Hobbes was 17th century.

"Yeah, I know. He was reading the line that said life is short and brutal. And he had to warn the class before he read that excerpt."

Naweed smiles faintly. "That's how it's become on campuses.

The day after Trump's election, (one of my) professors decided to make use of the session by having a period for grieving.

"Students were crying in class. And there was one student, she was wearing a hijab, she stood up and said, 'Professor, is it true that Trump's going to put my family in a concentration camp?'

"The teacher put his hand on his chest, and said, 'Yes, unfortunately, yes.'"

He shakes his head at the memory, still incredulous. "As a political science major, I'm definitely in the lion's den."

To get those A's, Naweed, do you ever just tell your profs what they want to hear?

He grins. "Yeah, I've become an expert in writing Marxist papers. I know the ideology."

How do these academics get around our historic commitment to free speech?

"Well, they believe in a concept called hate speech (as a rationale to override free speech). If you ask them where this hate-speech concept came from, and how do you define hate speech, and who is to regulate it, they never have an answer for you."

Hmmm. Let's see, now. Who would "volunteer" to be the censors? Let me guess...Yes—they would!

In one sense, Naweed is smarter than all the professors who try to indoctrinate students. Smarter, because he—not they—understands that the First Amendment is not only law, it's spiritual.

* * *

The visceral need to censor is a combination of arrogance and fear—arrogance that my ideas are superior; fear that they are not.

Orwell said freedom of speech is the right to say two plus two equals four. I go one step further. I say, it is the right to say two plus two equals five.

There are 1.5 million college teachers in the U.S. I ask at least one—please, just one—to make like a prophet of old and stand in the college quad and thunder—"You are betraying the principles that justify you being here!"

Taking free speech out of the university is like taking the cross out of the church.

San Diego Union-Tribune, August 21, 2017

This man dealt death—
and he was good at it

ADVISORY: This story contains adult imagery and language about warfare.

Sniper Chuck Mawhinney

The man is kneeling in the tall grass, unmoving as a lizard on a rock. He has learned the finesse of the expert killer, which is not to threaten but to lull.

He had been here for hours, since long before the blazing noonday sun rose slowly as a red ball to absorb the night chill. In his face-paint and artful camouflage, he doesn't exist.

The muscles of his young legs are locked into place without pain. When he moves, rarely, it is in slow motion, like a mime on valium. A drink of water takes minutes from when he reaches for his canteen. A leech is growing fat on the back of his neck, but he ignores it, knowing the creature will balloon with blood, then harmlessly fall off. Insects have worked inside his pants and shirt, but he blocks the itching from his mind.

Earlier, he observed a deadly krait from a few yards distant, but the snake crawled indifferently away, two predators taking a pass on each other. He sucks on granulated coffee from C-rats which he holds under his lip like Copenhagen, knowing the caffeine and bitter taste will help keep him alert. There is a companion hunched over about two feet from him, a togetherness each acknowledges with only a few secretive gestures and grunts, sometimes hours apart.

His eyes are fixed on a point far out in Indian Country, as this battle zone of Vietnam just below the DMZ is called. He ignores all else. A half-mile out in the middle of a rice paddy are ant-like dots. However, when he lifts his rifle and looks through the scope, the figures turn into three men dressed as farmers, apparently headed for a day's work. But the AK-47s they carry inadequately hidden reveal them as enemy soldiers—at least for a few more moments.

He looks expectantly at his spotter. The other man is absorbed in his binoculars, but senses the question, and answers in a single hushed word. "Clear." There are no other NVA in sight. He returns his eye to the scope and locks his brain into cruise control. He shifts the instrument from one man to another. They look alike, and all are fair game, but since he will allow himself only one shot, which one? God should be so arbitrary.

The scope is filled with the men, but he sees them as objectives, not as fellow humans. He doesn't look at their faces or their eyes. No point. This isn't personal. He notices one talking and the others listening. He looks more carefully at the soldier and sees that he carries a pistol at his side. Officers carry pistols. He is the one who will die today.

He settles the crosshairs on the man's chest—center mass. He estimates the distance…700 meters. His scope is sighted in on 500 meters, so he elevates the rifle slightly. The breeze on his cheek says the wind is about 12 mph. from the left. He moves the barrel slightly in that direction—maybe a quarter inch, but not three-eights. The death moment is now. He suspends breathing and gently tightens his finger. The stock slams into his shoulder, but he holds his head and grip just for a moment. Follow through. Tiger Woods. Michael Jordan. He is that kind of good.

His view suddenly empties. He shifts the scope and sees his target on the ground. Nothing moves except the seeping blood. The other two men look down, then around: stunned, then frantic.

They had heard nothing, but know death is keen-eyed and out there somewhere. He could easily kill both, but his own iron rule says otherwise—one shot, one kill.

Chuck Mawhinney, skinny 20-year-old sniper from the mountains of Oregon, and spotter Bob "Sugar Bear" Bryant, a burly black youth from inner-city Philadelphia, turn without a word and start back at a cautious but fast hunched-over trot to the Marine perimeter more than a half-mile distant. It has been a productive day. An average one for the Marine acknowledged as the most successful sniper of the Vietnam War.

* * *

Mawhinney is older now, 53, and he walks with a slight limp from a hip gone bad from first carrying 100 pounds of gear through rice paddies during the worst years of the war, '68 to '70, and then from years after of trying to make mountain roads passable for the U.S. Forest Service.

He is about six-two and rangy. He dresses in the casual practicality of the mountain man. His skin is leathered and clear. His eyes are always moving, not nervously, but in reaction to every motion, in the way of the lifelong hunter who always gets his deer.

He has a soft-spoken sandpaper sense of humor, but he rubs it in gently. He lives in an Eastern Oregon mountain town, the name of which he doesn't want printed because publicity still brings him occasional "child-killer" anonymous phone calls.

From the place where he now stands in his backyard, the Oregon Trail winds along just a few miles to the east, and it's easy for the imagination to transport him back to those pioneers of a century and a half ago. They would have known him. His whole manner says that he would rather take a beer piss into a snow bank at the foot of a tall pine with a skin-shrinking cold wind blowing through its lower branches, and then win a free trip to Disney World.

Mawhinney had been a teen-age hell raiser—"I liked to fight a little and race motorcycles, sometimes with cops chasing me." His enlistment was the alternative offered by a probation officer who persuaded authorities to give the wild kid an offer he couldn't refuse.

* * *

The old sniper is now retired from the Forest Service and has long-since become domesticated. At the moment he is worrying about a pork loin on the barbeque. If he wants a cigarette, he obediently leaves the house, and he watches how many Keystone Lutes he drinks.

For a quarter-century, his coworkers and neighbors knew nothing unusual about him: Just another good-guy neighbor, a blue-collar fellow with a modest house, a friendly wife and healthy kids. When he and his buddies would get together for beers on Fridays after work, he was the one who said nothing when the talk turned to war bragging.

"You'd get these guys who were in motor pools or supply back in DaNang, and they'd talk about their night missions, and bullshit like that. 'I was a bad sumbitch,' and all that stuff. I'd just sit and listen. If they asked me about the war, I'd just tell 'em I was lucky, I didn't get drafted." He is still amused by the ruse.

A few years ago, however, Mawhinney's years of silence about his war record came to an end in the pages of a paperback, "Dear Mom: A Sniper's Vietnam," written by Joe Ward, an ex-buddy in the same sniper platoon.

Ward identified Mawhinney as the top sniper in the entire war. As word of that revelation was circulated, his pals stopped telling war stories when he took a seat at the bar. A man who came back to Oregon with 103 confirmed kills and 216 probable kills might not be impressed.

There's always a question about such statistics. Who's counting? In Mawhinney's case, it was primarily his squad leader, Mark Limpic, now a 56-year-old engineer in Kansas City, Mo., but then the sergeant of a sniper squad in Vietnam. "How do I know how many confirmed kills he had? Because I counted them. Every one went in my book." On the probable kills, Limpic isn't certain, but said 216 might be low. "Generally, we figured at least two and maybe three probables to every confirmed," he said.

Of the skinny kid who followed his orders, Limpic says: "Chuck was an incredible shot and a guy who knew terrain like a wolf. Helluva Marine. He was the real deal."

* * *

Today, Mawhinney is trying to make the best of the notoriety that he didn't seek by teaching sniper skills to police department SWAT teams across the country, where he must seem like Ted Williams demonstrating how to hit a curve ball. He's suddenly in demand because the War on Terror has made heroes out of Special Operations soldiers, and SWAT-team snipers are no longer seen as psychopaths with means. He knows, as does every police officer, that the frontline of that war could erupt on the main street of any town in America.

Recognition has brought Mawhinney into uncomfortable proximity with sniper wannabes and hangers-on. He scoffs at the bravado slogans that make the rounds in that shadow world: "The only thing I feel is the recoil." "You can run, but you'll only die tired." "Can you see something like that on the side of a police car?" he asks, and shakes his head.

He tells of being invited to a sniper event in Las Vegas sponsored by "Soldier of Fortune" magazine. "There were these assholes walking around in camouflage with about six knives strapped to their bodies. One of them came up to me and said, 'Hey, man, you a sniper?' I said, 'No, man, I'm the caterer.' I got the hell out of there."

Mawhinney teaches cops the military skills that worked for him in Vietnam. He has the ardor of a TV preacher on the subject of practice time—and then more of it—the single quality that he calls the key to sniper success. "SWAT members on small departments have other duties, so they get out maybe once a month to shoot.

"That's bullshit. When I was In-Country, I practiced every day I wasn't out doing it. If you have to think about the steps you take to shoot, then you're not ready to shoot. Take these cops: they almost always have only one shot, so they have to know how their gun will react to cold-bore shooting. A cold barrel will throw the shot off by an inch or two. That can mean the difference on whether the one you kill is the one you want to kill."

Mawhinney scoffs at war stories, but if you're sitting with him in his garage hideaway with a couple Keystones, he can be coaxed to limber up.

He sets the scene in a well-documented incident: It happened on Valentine's Day 1969 on the Thu-Bon River near the Cambodia border. Mawhinney's company, operating out of the Liberty Bridge artillery base, had set up in the elephant grass about 400 yards from the water. An observation airplane had radioed that a large enemy force was moving toward them.

"I grab my spotter and an M-14 with a Starlight (night vision scope) and go down to the river bank to watch. We pick a place where the river is wider, because that means it's shallower at that point. We set up in high grass about 30 feet from the bank. About two hours after dark, one guy comes out of the river. No pack, only a rifle. I'm watching him. He looks around, then walks around for awhile. I can hear water dripping off him, that's how close he is. I don't shoot. I want to know what he's up to. Finally, he gets back in the river and disappears. I tell my spotter, 'This might get interesting.'

"Yep. About a half-hour later, here they come, wading across, a whole string of 'em. The water's up to their necks. They got those old green pith helmets on. As the first guy is coming out of the water, I shoot him, then go to the next one, then the next one, then the next. Like shooting fish in a bucket. I have the reticle right on their faces. Every shot a hit. Some would try to duck beneath the water, but what the hell's that gonna get 'em? These boys were screwed. They just floated away."

Later, Mawhinney counted the shells in that clip. Sixteen had been used, none wasted. The company enjoyed a peaceful bivouac that night.

* * *

It wasn't all target shooting. The NVA weren't clay pigeons. In addition to being wounded by shrapnel when another soldier blundered into a booby trap, Mawhinney spent an eternity one morning lying face down in the muck of a rice paddy.

"One day, I'm on patrol with the grunts and I get pinned down in this rice paddy. The furrow I'm in is maybe 10 inches deep and some asshole keeps shooting my pack because that's all he can see. So every time I move, I get hit again. The guy's in the tree line, maybe 30 feet away.

"The rice paddy is filled with shit—human—you know, but at that moment, I love shit more than a pretty girl, can't get close enough to it. He shoots me maybe half a dozen times. I can feel it in my shoulders; hurts like hell. Then, I feel something liquid running down my side. Sure as shit, I figure I've been hit. But I have three or four cans of peaches in my pack—I love peaches— and that son of a bitch hit a can. Finally, things got hot for the guy and he left. I just had to stay down tight and wait it out. Probably lasted a minute at most, but seemed like forever."

He shows me a photo of a kneeling figure in the far distance, obviously taken through a scope. "This guy, he's about 300 yards out. He's out there acting like a farmer, and at first we figure he's working, but then my spotter says, 'Chuck, he's got a rifle hidden in the grass.' End of story. Write your last letter, buddy. We were on the perimeter, and one Marine had a camera, so I put the camera up to the scope and turned it into a Kodak moment before I sent him home. When we went out there, we found that he'd been making a detailed sketch of our whole position."

The spotter's job was to use binoculars to scan a wider area and be ready with an M-14 or M-16 for "heavy lifting" if they were discovered and rushed. The spotter was also an apprentice sniper. Most graduated to the sniper role themselves, but some couldn't take the "scope-shot," as Mawhinney calls it. "Some guys are fine in a fire fight because it's kinda anonymous," he says, "but they just can't put a scope on one guy's face and blow it away."

Neophyte spotters could get you killed, and Mawhinney was not a gentle instructor. "One time it was getting dark and my dumb-ass rookie spotter had the Starlight scope on his M-14, and I didn't know he'd loaded his magazine with tracers. He opened up on some movement he saw, and it was like a red line pointing right to us. I grabbed him and we ran like crazy while the spot where we had just been blew all to hell. Afterwards, we had us a little counseling session about using tracers from a sniper position."

* * *

We're sitting in his garage lair, and a couple of neighbors drop by. The Keystones pop, and the laughter becomes freer. After going outside to take a whizz against a cottonwood, he's open to a request to show his gun collection. He leads the way into the house where his locked gun cabinet holds a place of honor. Next to it is an ornate frame holding a Bronze Star and Purple Heart, a gift from his family.

He displays his 20 or so guns the way a skilled carpenter would his tools or a surgeon his instruments. The place of honor is held by a duplicate of his bolt-action Remington .308 which was presented to him by the Corps. The original is locked away at Quantico where it someday will go into a Marine museum. He holds it cautiously out of habit, first checking the breech for maybe a forgotten round.

As he operates the bolt and scans for rust, memories return, and he talks of long nights along the tree line that turned into golden mornings, waiting for the dew to dry and watching the farmers leave their hooches and walk toward the fields. He was not fooled by bucolic scenes, however, and he watched for giveaway signs of booby traps, such as carefully skirted trails.

He's warmed up, and he segues into gun talk like an insurance guy into annuities. "I used 168-grain match ammo. It's gotta be match ammo, special made, because every bullet has to act just like the one before. My scope was a 3x9 Redfield. Like a Model-T Ford, now." He shows how the thick barrel of the gun is screwed into the receiver and "floats" above the stock.

He takes a piece of paper and slides it between the barrel and the wooden stock. "If the barrel was solid on the frame of the gun, the jarring would throw it off true. It's gotta be suspended. We didn't have these slick variable scopes, laser range finders, or some of the other stuff available to today's snipers, but we made do." He did make do.

The memories jump in his mind like popcorn. "Your senses get sharper over there because that's what you live by. First thing, your eyesight and hearing start picking up. You start keening in on stuff, especially at night. The whole country smelled to me like burnt bamboo. Can't explain it, but when that smell would change, no matter how small, I'd pick up on it.

"Here's something else: people stink. You usually don't realize it, but you do if your life depends on it, and you know it if someone's near. Fear even has a smell. For real. If I'd get a feeling something was wrong, I'd get my ass right back to camp. Maybe nothing was out there and maybe I was wrong, but I'm still alive."

Every step he took was cautious and every glance was suspicious. If a villager happened to observe his hide, he would abandon it. If a large enemy unit passed in the distance, he would refrain from taking a shot because of the fear of being caught by flankers; he would head back to call in an air strike.

"If I'm gonna be in a one-sided gunfight, I want the 'one' to be on my side." He didn't worry about the barking of village dogs. "Hell, a dog over there was a delicacy. It didn't last long. If a villager had three or four, he was a rancher.

"Sometimes, I could be out there all day and not take a shot, but it wasn't time wasted. I might go back to the company and tell the C.O., 'Hey, look, don't send a squad out there. You're gonna get into a helluva fight because there's a whole company of goddamned NVA setting up in that ville, and you go out there in squad strength, you're gonna get your boys killed.'"

* * *

Although snipers have played a role throughout American military history, from Daniel Morgan's Virginia backwoodsmen popping redcoats to rebel sharpshooters in the Devil's Den at Gettysburg, there is a psychological shadow that lingers over the soldier willing to make war so personal.

Dave Grossman is a man who has put military killing under a microscope. Author of "On Killing," and a retired army lieutenant colonel, he taught psychology at West Point and also graduated from Ranger school. "Killing as a sniper doesn't require a nut case eager to see blood. To the contrary, it requires a man with a strong sense of duty who is a quiet, introspective person comfortable with solitude and willing to act alone.

"As he gets older, he has to learn to be reconciled with his life, to make peace with the magnitude of what he's done—killed someone's child whose future is gone because he put a bullet in that stranger's heart or brain. Learning to live with that is made tougher because you can't talk it out the way other people do with ordinary problems. Can you imagine going to a community counselor and saying, 'I have an issue that's been bothering me—I killed 100 men....'? This is a search for self-understanding that takes a strong man."

* * *

If Mawhinney has bad nights over his sniper past, he conceals it well. "I shot over 300 people. I know that. I can't sweeten it up and say, 'Oh, I felt so bad every time I killed someone,' because I didn't. In my mind, I didn't take lives, I saved them. In the field, I'd think, 'If this one goes down, how many Marines are gonna live because of it?' That enemy out there is gonna kill me, if he can. So, if I'm first to the punch, that's good."

He has no desire to join some other combatants in a pilgrimage back to Vietnam to find reconciliation. "Why should I go back? I didn't leave anything there."

In a lot of ways, he loved it. After serving his mandatory year In-Country, he re-up'd for two six-month tours. "This'll sound kinda funny, but I love to hunt. Always have. People can say, 'Man, we're going to Africa and hunt lions, hunt cape buffalo, like it was the scariest thing ever. But to me, when you're hunting another man who has a weapon of his own, now that's hunting the baddest thing you can ever hunt. For 16 months as a sniper I was on the ultimate hunt."

* * *

Mawhinney is at his calmest driving through his beloved Blue Mountains. After pointing out from his jostling pickup where elk herds run, he says quietly, "You can't kill that many men and not think about it. I do, every day. But I always come back to the truth that I never killed a single man who wasn't trying to kill me." His thoughts and conversation wander, the way it does when a man is at peace in his surroundings.

Suddenly, we pass an area that reminds him of the days he used to earn Christmas money by trapping fur animals in the winter snow. "Not too long ago, I was checking my line, and there was this sorry old bastard of a coyote caught in one of my traps. When I came up on him, he gave me this pitiful look like, 'I'm in so damned much misery, why don't you just shoot me?' I did; had no choice. Then I gathered up my traps and put them away. For good."

Penthouse Magazine, 2003

Infant girl is saved from abandonment, then earns college

Hannah Flagg

Societies can't resist doing stupid and tragic things. That's why history is more interesting than reality TV.

In China, until last year, a dim-bulb idea had been clicked on to limit families to one child to reduce population. Well, that's one bureaucratic program that worked. Millions of baby girls were aborted, given up as orphans, or abandoned for the simple(ton) reason they weren't boys.

(The consequence for China has been a minority of very picky women and a big surplus of horny men.)

Such a great number of baby girls were discarded that mobile patrols drove the streets to pick them up.

Government policies are normally examined with impersonal analytical detachment, but the human effect they have is lived by individuals, one by one.

In the South China city of Guangzhou there likely is a woman who sometimes interrupts her day to grieve for a tiny baby, the days-old girl she surrendered or had torn from her arms on a December day 17 years ago. The baby was placed on a park bench to be found or to die.

That new-born was found, and is doing just fine now as Hannah Flagg, a college-bound superior student with a great future tucked among the books in her backpack.

* * *

Hannah is a petite, cute girl with a toothy smile and none of the social hesitancy of many teens. Her manner is matter-of-fact, but when she talks of the beast that also lived in her San Marcos, Calif. home, her eyes rim with red.

The evil presence in that household made Hannah an orphan a second time.

* * *

In the fall, Hannah will matriculate at UCLA on full-ride scholarships where she will study the sciences. She will mingle with rich kids and foreign students who made it there because someone had the money to cross international borders or pay for tutors.

Hannah calculates she will have about $1,000 to $2,000 left over for the entire school year to pay for everything beyond fees, housing and books. That's in expensive Westwood. The guy who takes her on a date better be ready to pick up the tab.

However, if that guy has the curiosity to ask, and the patience to listen, he will hear a story of childhood heartache and gritty perseverance that will be educational beyond hamburger chit-chat and a movie.

*   *   *

Hannah was adopted, along with another, unrelated Chinese girl a year older, who was found on a street corner and also rescued by Peter and Donna Flagg of San Marcos. Hannah remembers them as kind, loving parents to the girls, and painfully loving to each other. It could have been a storybook family—love conquering distance and culture—except for one thing; one nasty, irreparable, unconquerable thing:

Alcoholism, raging and uncontrollable.

Hannah remembers, "We had what seemed like a normal family: nice house, nice neighborhood, nice school. Mom was a stay-at-home mom, involved in PTA and what not. It wasn't until I was maybe 7 that I kind of started to realize that things weren't normal. I knew they drank, but I didn't know the consequences of it. My mom would be hiding alcohol in a closet, and me and my sister would be finding it."

The girls' father was a former salesman who in 2004 opened a sandwich and bagel shop in San Marcos. It went under in 2008. He didn't work thereafter. The family lived on welfare and a grandmother's assistance. Slim living, especially when booze is atop the shopping list, above milk and eggs.

"My dad was what people would call a functioning alcohol. He could drink and drink, and be drunk, and you wouldn't notice because he was still able to do his job."

Ah, but what the girls had to witness, day and night: "They would fight. They would never touch us girls, but there were a lot of nights when my mom would drink, and she would get really, really drunk. My dad would also be drinking, but it was less noticeable.

"My mom, when she would drink, she would turn violent. She would go after my dad and start screaming at him and punching him. He would push her away, and because she was so out of it, she would fall down, and have bruises on her. They would be screaming at each other, throwing things.

"I remember, distinctly, one night she threw a hot iron at my dad, and he had an iron burn on his arm. Sometimes police would show up. It wasn't uncommon for Child Protective Services to come and kind of ask us questions. We always covered up because we didn't want to be taken away.

"There was this one night it got so bad that my dad took me and my sister out of the house. He just grabbed sleeping bags from our garage. We slept in a parking lot because we couldn't be in the house."

Let's perhaps soften our judgment somewhat as we remember this was a couple that reached all the way to China for two tiny abandoned humans whose lives would have been otherwise hopeless.

These two, Peter and Donna, they had their dreams, and they had love, and they did their best for their daughters. Of course, that alcohol sickness had to be taken care of first. That's what it requires. It's a nasty, demanding house guest that won't go home.

Peter and Donna must have done a lot right, because they took two babies still almost warm from the womb and turned them into admirable young women; certainly Hannah, the one of my brief acquaintance.

Hannah says she has no curiosity about her birth parents. She doesn't think about them or about the mystery of her beginnings. She is grateful to be where she is and with her life as it is.

Hannah has a flash in her black eyes that's all business, but a caring, compassionate side takes over when she talks of the parents who made her a prisoner-witness to an adults' world of pain and rage.

"I loved them very much. Very much. They had all these problems, but they were still my parents. You know, honestly, even after all that, they were still the best parents I could ask for. I wouldn't change anything, because I wouldn't be the person I am without them."

Were they apologetic and remorseful?

"Yes. I know that neither of them wanted to drink. My mom had been to rehab several times. My dad would go to meetings and stuff. It's not like they wanted to do it, but once you get set on that track, it's hard to stop.

"They tried hard. They had been doing it for so long that their bodies had just become dependent on it, and it's hard to stop that. My dad would get seizures when he didn't drink."

The inevitable happened in 2010 when Donna, age 52, was admitted to the hospital: sclerosis of the liver, no surprise. Hanna was only 11 so it was all a mystery to her. Her mother was rarely conscious, so there was no chance for a mother-daughter talk.

When death came, "I didn't believe it at first. Yeah. I was reading a book, because we all were just sitting there. My mom wasn't conscious. All of a sudden, all her machines just started beeping. All these doctors came in. My thought was—What's going on?

"Then, all of a sudden, they were like—Oh, she's dead. She's gone. I think both my sister and I were just, like—What just happened? We hadn't even known she was really dying.

"It was kind of like—What do you mean she's gone? She was just here. I just saw her heart thing going up and down. Then they started disconnecting all the machines. I was crying."

Then the long trip home: two young girls and a drunken father.

"My dad, he tried really hard. He continued to drink even worse because he fell into pretty heavy depression. He was taking pills for it. I know that the only thing keeping him together was my sister and me. He tried as hard as he could. He was trying to go to meetings. He was trying to stop, but he couldn't.

Last year, the disease came for Peter. Admitted to the hospital with liver failure one day, he was dead the next morning. He was also 52.

Life for the young has a strong bounce-back. Hannah and her sister, Cassie, became wards of an uncle in Long Beach where

Cassie is now in college. Hannah is living with God-parents locally as she wraps up her senior year.

Hannah continued her pursuit of excellence, which for her was not a hard catch.

"School is very easy," she says with typical candor. "I honestly don't have to try. I don't have to do the homework or study. I don't think I've really ever studied for a test or anything."

That's about to change at UCLA, Hannah.

She will graduate on Wednesday from Mission Hills High School in San Marcos with a GPA higher than straight-A.

She augmented her average by taking advanced placement classes and with community service. She served 3 years on the San Marcos Youth Commission and was active as a Red Cross volunteer.

Right now, there's no June gloom for Hannah. If bad things continue to just leave her alone, we can expect in a few years to see a woman of accomplishment who will give to society far more than she could ever take. Don't be surprised to someday see "Hannah Flagg, M.D." She wouldn't.

To that guilt-ridden woman in China, I wish I could say— Your baby is doing quite well. I'm sorry you won't see what your daughter will become.

San Diego Union-Tribune, June 20, 2016

ALS knows no pity and always wins in the end

John and Lin Constans

John Constans looks at his hands in sorrow. They no longer have the strength to trim a 737 jetliner or repair the water heater in the family garage: achievements that made John proud because he did them well, both large and small.

John loved his life's work as a Navy pilot, PSA pilot, captain for U.S. Airways, and then as simulator instructor passing his skill on to young pilots.

That's gone.

John's life was as co-head of household with his wife, Lin, and father of two grown daughters, enjoying the leadership and duties of an active, involved dad and husband.

That's gone.

John is a gentle, kindly man with a supportive family and is a steady, reliable guy with many friends, especially from his flying days.

That remains.

* * *

John has had his life invaded—actually, taken over—by a motor neuron disease that has no known cause, but an unavoidable end. Its name is ALS. If you're up on such things, you might call it amyotrophic lateral sclerosis, or you certainly know it by its more chilling name—Lou Gehrig's disease.

The usual pattern of the disease leads rapidly to muscle weakness of the limbs, also muscle twitching and cramping, thickening speech and difficulty of swallowing and breathing. Drugs are of little value. At any given time, 30,000 adult Americans suffer from it, men and women. ALS is not contagious.

By any name, it is a torment with no cure. It leads the patient down a dark path to a respirator and paralysis of the entire body except the eyes. But the mind—the mind remains aware. And then, after a few years, death.

These are grim words, I know, but what other would you have me use that measures what John is facing? I am not going to sugarcoat his struggle, just as he determines not to do. I know these words do not shock him because he thinks of them every day. He knows them by heart. One does not diminish horror by refusing to speak its name.

The first day of the rest of John's life was in July 2011. He couldn't ignore worrisome signs that had grown more insistent over six months. The problem first caught his attention that January. While vacationing in Hawaii he discovered that swimming was strangely exhausting. Puzzled, he dragged himself from the surf, then reminded himself he was, after all, 66. He shrugged and forgot it.

But he gradually grew weaker and was often out of breath. Fatigue became troublesome. Certainly, nothing near alarming, but enough to go in for tests. He underwent a lengthy diagnosis, then, finally, the results were in.

His wife, Lin, tells what then happened. "I learned later that they (doctors) have a protocol for these things: it should be the last appointment of the day, and that all other patients would be taken care of and out of the way. There is a certainly way you're told things, but it's delivered straight.

"(The doctor) said, 'This is what you have, and it's progressive, and generally the life expectancy is three to five years. I just think you would want me to be truthful with you.'"

Lin continued, "When the doctor started talking about it, I can remember grabbing John's hand. With the other, I was digging my fingers in. We were in shock.

"Walking back to the car, John said, 'ALS. You know that's what Lou Gehrig died of.'

"'Yeah,' was all I could say."

John's mind froze at the news. "I was stunned. I had no clue. No clue. How could this be? What the hell!" But after a confirming diagnosis, and further degeneration, he had to accept the truth.

And as the doctors had told them, it started. Slowly at first, but everything worsened with the dulling certainty of a metronome.

It's a disease that attacks the whole family, and must be fought by all. Red eyes are common in the house. Lin has geared up for the duration. She is John's caregiver, and she's practical about it.

"I think maybe I've gone back into 'mom' mode, taking care of all the little things for those dependent on you. As he can do less, I have just to do more. And so far I've been able to handle it. The physical part sometimes gets to me. I think I just ignored household repairs and things because I knew he was so good at it, but now he can't do it—like picking up heavy things, things that go wrong in the house."

* * *

This is not a Pollyanna script. As Lin takes on functions that formerly were John's, and hustles to keep atop her real estate business, there is occasional impatience and frustration. She tells of changing a vacuum cleaner belt while he instructed. It did not go well, either mechanically or emotionally. But they understand that as roles shift, and Lin becomes more in charge, hurt feelings are bound to occur, but will quickly pass.

Lin's gritty steadfastness has deepened John's appreciation of his wife. His voice doesn't sound quite so labored as he says, "She's stepped up, big time…big time."

Fortunately, they have avoided most of the usual money squeeze that goes with the disease because of excellent insurance, and medical care from the VA which both praise lavishly.

* * *

It's June, and John can no longer easily stroll around their comfortable home, modest by the standards of the upscale San Diego suburb of Rancho Santa Fe where they live. John spends hours now sitting in a soft recliner, but he can find little comfort. He often twitches and twists to find a better position and ease muscle cramps. Behind him, past the glass patio door, is the swimming pool that means nothing to him now and is no longer heated. The family dog, a weird-looking, lovable little combo pug and terrier, has commandeered a spot next to John's feet for napping.

John says he can still drive a car, his coordination is fine, but his hand strength has so diminished that he has to turn-on the ignition key with pliers. "A year ago I was clueless. Had some minor issues with the disease, but doing okay, overall. Now I get it.

Breathing is a real issue, as well as walking, eating and speaking. Simple tasks are becoming more and more difficult. I can feel my body slowly shutting down."

In July, the progress of his disease has pushed ahead with the methodical pace of a trotting dog. "This week I got fitted for a power wheelchair. I can still cut my food and swallow, but I'm starting to eat more like a toddler than an adult." His neck muscles are weakening to the point where he sometimes has to reach up and push back his slumping head.

He is in discomfort from the recent surgical implant of a feeding tube in his stomach. He has lost 30 pounds, mainly muscle mass, and the doctors want him to work toward regaining the weight. He is on a diet of 2,600 calories and he can't possible ingest that amount by his laborious eating, hence the feeding tube. Looking back on the tube implanting, John only says, in his laconic manner, "That was a tough one to handle."

He can't escape reminders "I saw (physicist and ALS sufferer) Stephen Hawking on TV. He was in a motorized wheelchair and the only thing that moved were his eyes...scary."

* * *

The Constans' daughters, Ashley, 30, and Elise, 24, celebrated last Christmas at home as though nothing had happened. And nothing had. The parents elected to save the bad news for later.

Two days after Christmas, the daughters were shopping when they got a call to come home for a family conference. Elise remembers, "I asked what was up, and dad said, 'You know what, guys? It's not good.'"

Both women joined the team. Elise moved back from Italy to assist at home, and Ashley has helped organize fund-raisers for ALS, as has Lin.

It's August, and John is more aware of time and the value of it. Weeks, days, hours...but just as he savors them, he's more aware of their passing. He spends a lot of time thinking who he is and who he has been. He reads some and watches a little TV, but it's difficult to stay in one position for long.

"Its funny, when I go to sleep at night, I think about certain stages of my life, and what was I doing when I made this or that decision. It kind of gives me some peace. When I replay my life, I tend to go past the bad parts, the stupid stuff I did."

He says he quickly becomes nostalgic, almost maudlin some-times, as when he bursts into tears at the sound of a familiar song or seeing a favorite movie. His thoughts, inexplicably, sometimes drift to the memory of listening to a Steppenwolf song, "Born to be Wild," while in a holding pattern over a carrier off Vietnam.

He yearns to visit his boyhood home in Twain-Harte, a small town in the Northern California Gold Country. He is aiming to attend his 50th high school reunion in Sacramento in the fall.

"I think I've pretty much made amends with everybody I think I've pissed off," he says with a smile.

Last January, John had to give up a job he enjoyed, teaching young pilots in a simulator for Boeing. He also could no longer deliver jets to distant destinations, something he relished in recent years. He truly loved flying. He loved planes, he loved his crew, he loved the sky. He even loved passengers. He loved all of it.

I ask John how he is doing on the Kubler-Ross five-step stages of grief continuum, going from denial to acceptance. His dry humor flashes: "I guess I'm at acceptance. Denial didn't do me much good." Then, he adds, "You can only say 'why me' so many times."

John says he tries to talk to Lin about his no longer being with her. "She says it's not time to talk about that. She's more about keeping me going, not giving up."

* * *

As summer turns to September, I can see the pain in his face as he twists his body in the chair, trying to escape discomfort.

John bleakly tells me of his greatest despair, his morning prepara-
tions. "Before, I could shave and tie my shoes. Now, it's an issue.
Showering is a pain. I have to think about putting my feet into
my undershorts and then my pants, and then getting my t-shirt
on. Then I have to sit down because I'm tired. Every small daily
function takes a lot of effort. I get tired having to work to breathe.
If I get up from a chair wanting to do something, I'm already tired
from just getting up. Normal daily activity is down to–how can I
survive the day?"

The thought of eventually depending on others, even strangers,
for help in the most basic, intimate bodily functions bothers him
greatly.

"Much of the time my survival mechanism is my sense of
humor, which I'm using more and more these days. However, as
I look in the mirror I can definitely see the effects of the disease. I
see a refugee from a concentration camp. Deep inside, I'm scared."

Family things that have to be decided range from the mundane
to the profound. Lin says, "We have to start thinking now about
a van to be able to accommodate the wheelchair. John's talking
about finding a place in Rosecrans (military cemetery) to be
buried. He wants to do that and maybe get a headstone."

At the end of a lengthy conversation, I ask Lin what she most
fears. Her eyes fill and her voice lowers. "That he might suffer."
Then, I ask what causes her to be hopeful. Her lip quivers and she
looks down. "Nothing."

I ask John—as gently as I can—if he has had thoughts of
suicide. He chuckles, and says that is the first thing his counselor
at the VA always asks him. "I think about it, but I don't see myself
doing that. I can see why someone would go down that road, but
I don't want to do it. I just have too much support, and personally,
my legacy, especially with my daughters, I wouldn't want to mess
that up."

Asked about his thoughts on religion, John says, "I was raised
in a formal church, but I've drifted away from that approach to
a more self-directed spirituality…Yes, I pray to God and ask for

strength to get through each day…Man, have things changed. I wonder what's on the other side. I hope there's something, but, who knows?"

* * *

It's October when I next see John, but the man who answers the door seems shrunken from the one I visited just a short time ago. John's chin almost rests on his chest because of weakened neck muscles, and his arms and legs show little flesh below sagging skin. The short trip to the door leaves him gasping for breath.

He is becoming more and more homebound. "Don't get out much, now," he says. The high school class reunion in Sacramento didn't happen, and the trip to the boyhood home in Twain-Harte is not going to. "That's okay," John says, "I've got good memories."

He is coming off a disappointing trip into the operating room. Doctors wanted to strengthen his diaphragm to improve his breathing, but when they checked him arthroscopically, they discovered the diaphragm was not strong enough to receive the implant. The plan failed. Recovering from surgery, he had an attack of ileus, an intestinal blockage that gave him what Lin says was "incredible pain" for several days.

He is almost totally nourished by his feeding tube now, as doctors try to load him with calories to forestall weight loss. Outside is a van modified for a wheelchair patient. It has been loaned by the family of an ALS patient that doesn't need it anymore. I let the meaning of that speak for itself.

When it comes time to leave, I tell him I can let myself out, but he struggles to his feet and walks me to the door.

I look back toward the door and see not the same John Constans as in previous months, except for one thing: He's still hanging tough.

* * *

How do you measure a man's life? Well, I don't think you do. Only he and his family can do that, and ultimately, just himself. And, for John, that is what he values of what remains, time to make love glow and character strong. For that opportunity he is grateful for every day left to him.

John knows he is heading into the unknown, a trip all must make, but each must make alone as supporting hands slip away.

John Constans is not a man who would attract attention on an average street. He is, like almost all of us, a resident of his own space and his own castle. When his day comes, he will be missed by his many friends, his aviation family, and his family of hearth and home; also, namelessly, by many thousands of travelers who were grateful every time the wheels kissed the tarmac gently. In all those years, not one of them failed to deplane safely. Not one. If he leaves any enemies, they are now in deep cover.

He will leave behind only his legacy, and that is what he is trying to shape with fading strength. Already the framework of that legacy is clear. It will be of a man who found his work useful and rewarding, who gave his friends and country loyalty and his family love. It will be of a man who looked this ugly disease in the face, and said, "I will not win, but the only thing of value you will take from me is life."

John normally ends his emails with the circled happy face. I know it's a cliché, but to John it means goodwill and good cheer.

That's the way John Constans ends things.

(John Constans died in 2014.)

San Diego Union-Tribune, October 15, 2012.

A comic looks for a laugh and finds a life

Dave Wright

It's 6 p.m. on a Friday and thousands of San Diegans have someplace to be, or are headed there. But only about 15 are at Winston's bar in Ocean Beach, California to catch the comics during open-mike time.

Winston's is not where Jerry Seinfeld hangs out. But—hold on—it's just like places where Seinfeld once did, back when Jerry was just a guy with a joke and a hope. And that comic's dream is what motors our story.

Holding the mike at the moment, doing his five-minute shtick before he turns it over to the next five-minuter, is a short guy with the baritone pipes of a radio jock spieling, some funny lines. His name is Dave Wright, and you can't catch him on cable TV.

Halfway through his routine, a mouthy drunk with an early start begins interrupting with slurred and stupid comments to Wright. The guy is sitting on a stool next to his mostly sober girlfriend.

This is not a fair fight.

"Sir, I would guess you're a happy drunk. Is that true?"

"Yeahhhh."

"Tell me: Do you realize that EVERYONE is really pleased when you get drunk?"

The guy gives that idiotic, pointless drunk laugh.

"I think I know why. Because with that beer glass in your mouth you shut the hell up. Everyone in here would like you to have another beer."

The guy mutters on.

"Sir, please keep drinking so I can take your beautiful girlfriend home while you're face down in the men's room. Trust me, she'll thank you for it later."

Wright's indignation is feigned, because he secretly welcomes the encounter. Comics appreciate drunks the way cats appreciate mice: First to be played with, then devoured.

The others in the audience are gleeful when a drunk becomes a foil—it's someone else stepping up to play the fool. And, for this night, at least, it's not them.

Wright turns away from the drunk and slings one joke after another at the small crowd who either laugh approvingly or walk toward the bar or the washroom.

"A lot of people ask me if doing stand-up comedy is tough. I've had tougher jobs. I used to do door-to-door sales. I sold 'no soliciting' signs."

Winston's on this night is where Wright shows up for work, his tool box filled with fresh jokes, prepared again to joust with his dreams. He would prefer a guest spot on "The Tonight Show."

To Wright, and other striving-struggling comics, Winston's and other venues is either a stepping stone or a tombstone. For him, open-mike is like batting practice: he just wants to keep his swing smooth. He normally gets an 8 pm slot at the Comedy Store or the Mad House Comedy Club. At age 40 he's considered a step-up on most of the other open-mikers who tend to be—and this is a terrible thing to say about a comic—not very funny.

Wright came to San Diego from Delaware in 2000. He was without a car, so he rented a small place in La Jolla for $700, then got a job at a nearby restaurant. "It was me and my dog and a bunch of money, and the money ran away."

He met a girl during one of his early routines and invited her out to a bar near his home because he didn't want to admit he was carless. The date clicked and he ended up taking her home on the handlebars of his bike.

"I thought, I've come full circle: I'm in my late 20s and I've got a girl on my handlebars, just like high school. One of the things she liked about me was that she was able to tell her mom she was dating a comic. Her mom had only seen one comic and that was Larry the Cable Guy, so her mom kept going, 'Oh, you're dating a Larry the Cable Guy.'"

Day-time, Wright earns an actual living as an admissions counselor for an online university; a job on which quip opportunities are presumably few.

"The message 'coexist' should not be used as a bumper sticker. It's hard for me to support your cause in the middle of traffic. I'm in traffic! That's the place where I least care about other humans."

Wright says of his companions in comedy: "Comedy people are probably the weirdest, most unique, and in the same respect, most beautiful people that I've met in my life. We all have a unique view on how we see things. We all are a little twisted."

How about the cliché that comics are sad and insecure people?

"Yeah. There's a lot of truth to that. What I portray on stage is not who I am. I'm a very confident person on stage because I'm comfortable with the surroundings. I know how to get in and out of situations.

"I think it's a matter of, this makes me feel good about my sad life for a moment, if I talk about it in front of other people. Well, I don't really have a sad life, but I'm definitely not doing what I thought I'd be doing. I thought I'd be married by now, have a couple kids, and a house with a white picket fence."

"Young women are fun, but I want a woman who's lived a little: a woman who's made so many bad choices she understands that this—me—ain't so (bleeping) bad!"

How much money do you make as a comic?

"Oh, not much at all, very little. I never got into this primarily to make money. I got into this because I love it and because I'm a little sick in the head."

What's your ambition?

"To get good. To get to the point where I can make a career out of this. That to me would be heaven on earth."

"I used to write my jokes on my hand. Yeah, great trick. Then I went to the bathroom and I started to laugh at myself."

Are you thick- or thin-skinned?

"On stage, I'm thick. Off stage, thin—about where I am in life, about what I want to be when I grow up, about how much money I have, about relationships that I'm in or not in."

What is your purpose in comedy?

"My purpose? To make drunk people laugh. That's really it. I'm not trying to change the world. I don't want my words to inspire others to go off and climb a mountain or do great things and…come on, you're drunk. The drunker you are, the easier I'll get a good laugh from you."

"When I was a kid, my porn was National Geographic and Benny Hill ('80s TV slapstick comedy). Yep. I got off on an old man chasing women in bras and panties."

Just after delivering that line, he notices a young black woman in the audience enjoying herself, so he picks up on the National Geographic thing and directs his wit at her. He asks if she were dressed in a grass skirt and topless, would she mind teenage boys lusting and leering at her photo.

Sitting in the corner, I become a little tense and think, Oh, boy…The woman, however, laughs robustly.

He knows that such repartee is risky, but watches his audience and tries to select receptive members. And he's always ready to back off.

"I know I've worked too many bar gigs when I flush the toilet at mom's house with my foot."

Wright knows he's almost a senior citizen among local comics, but he's not age-obsessed. He points out that most big-time comics don't arrive on the big stage until middle age. He believes that a comic's portfolio is enriched by life experiences that only come with time.

"My goal in comedy is to be good. That's first and foremost. I enjoy the feeling of coming down off a stage, having entertained a group of people, and having that high.

"I just want to make people laugh."

San Diego Union-Tribune, September 16, 2013

A man suffering from cancer takes control of his life

Howard Wildfang

Howard l. Wildfang makes it a point to stay busy while he waits to die. He has been a man of determination for all his 85 years, and when his sickness finally closes its circle, he will quit life on his own terms.

He sits in his Salem, Ore., retirement-home apartment in a straight-back chair pulled close to the table. His papery skin is mottled. His body is shrunken. His words are reedy and pushed out with great effort, but his mind is alert as he organizes the tabletop. Strewn on it are newspapers and magazines he would like to read. Clamped to the table at the end of a metal arm is a round magnifying glass, big as a saucer. Drawing it close to his eye is the only way he can read because he has a degenerative eye disease.

It's a mean thing for a man who loves ideas. He grasps the glass with hands misshapen by rheumatoid arthritis and a deterioration of the tendons in his thumbs. They are locked at mid-joint at a 90-degree angle backward. One finger is only a stub, most of it lost to a sawmill blade years before. For someone who made his way in life with the strength of his arms—farmer, laborer, carpenter—it must be a hopeless thing to look down on crippled hands.

During the past dozen years, Wildfang has had three minor strokes and three operations for bladder cancer, which was not life-threatening but added to his health burdens. Last Aug. 29, Dr. Paul Munson called in his patient and friend of 30 years with unhappy news. An X-ray showed that the pain Wildfang had complained about was a 7-centimeter mass in a lung. There was little chance it wasn't cancerous. Both knew the old man couldn't long fight off such an attack.

What Munson didn't know was how defiant Wildfang already was at the prospect of a lingering death.

In the month after seeing Munson, Wildfang had a CT scan, which confirmed the tumor, then a CT-guided needle biopsy, which identified it as "squamous cell carcinoma," a nasty and ambitious cancer. He also met with Salem oncologist Charles Petrunin and radiation oncologist Nancy Boutin. Petrunin determined that chemotherapy wouldn't help Wildfang, and might kill him. Boutin was more optimistic and began radiation therapy at the beginning of October. It lasted all month, interrupted by a brief bout of pneumonia.

Boutin says she is pleased that the tumor has stopped growing and hopes that the radiation treatment will give Wildfang several more months. But it is clear the cancer is not going away. "The tumor is high up in the lung, up against the chest wall, causing him pain," she says. "Mr. Wildfang's cancer is one that doesn't spread to other parts of the body as quickly as other types. The radiation is not likely to cure him, but I'm hopeful it'll buy him some quality time. I suspect, when he dies, he will still have this cancer, whether he dies of it or of one of the many other things that 85-year-old men die of."

* * *

Wildfang says he submitted to radiation only to please his family, and he's resigned to his death, sooner or later. Sooner can be a few weeks, later can be several months.

"Sometimes now I just can't seem to get my thoughts together, and I feel like an idiot," he says. "Sometimes my words come out funny. It's been that way since my last stroke. But that's not the me I want remembered."

This is not a complaint. His doctors say he never complains. Wildfang is the product of a German-Scandinavian heritage in which grit is valued above style, and strength is best expressed as silent and unflinching. Like most of his generation, the Great Depression scarred his psyche. He learned that hard work and guarding dimes as if they're diamonds are the only means of pushing back poverty.

As the days stretch through November, he endures the cancer with painkillers, but he has no appetite, and his low weight leaves him vulnerable to infection. He grows increasingly apprehensive about what is to come. He thinks often of his first wife, Vivian, who died in 1975 of heart disease after months of pain-filled lingering that wore on her and the family. He thinks of his second wife, Georgia, who lost a son to cancer only a year ago, and of his four middle-aged children who also can't forget Vivian's death. What is he about to put them through? He does not want his passing to be a burden lifted.

"I know everyone in the family will say they'll take care of me, and all that, but why should I take advantage of the love they have for me?" he asks. "Psychologists say, 'Well, you grow closer together.' But the way I see it, it's their generosity and my selfishness. They may be willing to suffer through with me, but why should I let them? Watching me deteriorate would take a lot out of them that I don't want to see them give up."

Wildfang makes the loneliest and most personal decision of his 85 years. He will take his own life.

He has been thinking about it since Munson told him of the chest tumor. That he can even contemplate such an act is the result of an Oregon initiative that took effect in October 1997. The Death With Dignity law says that, with stipulated safeguards, any person with a disease diagnosed as terminal within a probable six months has the right to hasten death.

Wildfang also is driven by another impulse. He comes out of the rural Great Plains tradition that fostered much of the social and economic progressivism of American history. Through his death, he sees another way he can serve in that same populist spirit by showing others that they can control their lives right up to the end. That's why he has agreed that I can spend these days at his side or on the telephone with him. He wants to show others that there is a way to negotiate an honorable peace with death.

"Sometimes, late at night, I wake up and think about dying, and how it's going to happen. I know they can keep me doped up and all that, but I don't want to get to the point of being of no use to myself or anybody else. Life always reaches the point where it's time to pass on. Nowadays, we're often forced to live so much longer than nature intended; we stay beyond our time. I know from being around elderly neighbors that they worry about losing control near the end.

"It's bad enough to have to face death, but it's worse if we have to imagine ourselves just wasting away to where we don't amount to much more than something to pity. And suicide's not the answer. Why should I have to take a gun and commit violence as my last act on earth? Death With Dignity gives me the right to control my life right up to the end. And if I can do something that'll help other people realize that they can . . . well, maybe die a little better, then that's the memory that I'd rather leave with my family."

Dying is a far more wrenching thing than simply setting an example for others. Wildfang has his haunting moments. Those who say an 85-year-old should be ready to die are not 85. He blanches as he tells me that his rheumatologist and eye specialist both canceled further appointments with him. Their point: Why bother? He knows that's true, but it's still a slash to his psyche. When I ask if he just wants to get it over with, his eyes flash. "No. I want to live as long as possible." But a moment later, his head sinks: "Possible" is beyond wishful thinking.

* * *

In mid-November, Wildfang approaches Petrunin to help with his assisted death. The doctor hesitates. Like many Oregon physicians, Petrunin does not oppose assisted death, but neither is he comfortable being part of it. He refers Wildfang to his partner and fellow oncologist, Peter Rasmussen, a strong advocate of the law.

When Wildfang sits down with Rasmussen on Nov. 21, he wants to know how the disease will work its will on him. The physician tells him that his cancer can go in several directions. For smokers, as Howard had been for 70 years, pulmonary problems are common because the lungs have been weakened. The usual result for those patients is pneumonia, from which someone Wildfang's age usually doesn't recover. Also, the cancer can metastasize to bones, causing severe pain, or the brain, which can lead to nausea, behavioral changes and disorientation. Finally, the cancer can spread to a metabolic organ such as the liver or kidneys, a process that tends to be gradual and relatively gentle. The doctor tells Wildfang that, as the end nears, he can be kept sedated and on painkillers; in effect, kept in a coma and allowed to starve to death.

Wildfang rejects that alternative because, as he says later, "I guess I wouldn't feel anything, but my family would have to stand around the bed day after day and watch me shrink away. Why? What's the point in that?" He ends his meeting with Rasmussen determined as ever to, as he keeps repeating, "keep control."

Rasmussen is a quiet, kindly man of 58. He says Wildfang understands what is to come, but seems strong in the face of it. The doctor is struck that Wildfang wants his death to show others that life can be controlled to the end. "Howard is unique in that he's still interested in the big picture. He still cares what happens in Iraq," Rasmussen says. "As most patients get closer to death, their world cracks. Their interests contract down to, 'Who do I want to have around me today?' "

The physician outlines the steps the assisted death law requires: The patient must make verbal and written requests, and must wait at least 15 days before obtaining a prescription for the fatal dose: 10 grams of pentobarbital in a drinkable solution, about triple the amount necessary to kill an average adult. A psychiatric examination is not required unless one of the two physicians who must sign off as a final safeguard deem it necessary. The key to the process, which separates it from Dr. Jack Kevorkian-style assisted dying, is that the patient must self-administer the drug. The glass must be taken in hand and swallowed by the patient without assistance, although Rasmussen says that whether a family member can guide or steady the hand seems to be an untested gray area.

Of the patients who inquire about assisted death, about 10 per cent carry it out, he says. Some decide later to allow nature to take its own time, and for many others, death gets there first.

* * *

Now, barely into December, Wildfang waits, and thinks. He worries that his wife will have to struggle financially. He welcomes the chance to talk about what his life has meant, what he has done with it and what he has left undone. He is concerned that he has not influenced the world in the way he wanted, and he knows the chance to do so is fading. The centerpiece of his mission is a self-published book titled, "The Perfect Triangle: A Common Man's Philosophy," written during the course of a decade in his later years. It outlines his belief that society is gravely threatened by the excesses of corporate greed, corruption and lack of Christian social compassion. The book is homespun and not academic, but cogently reasoned and clearly written. It is not angry, only sad. His arguments are similar to those heard often in the Grange and farm-union halls of rural America 50 to 100 years ago, but they still hold currency today.

Wildfang had 500 of his books printed several years ago and has given them away to spread his beliefs. He has about 200 books remaining, and it's vital that as many as possible be given away before he dies. His wife Georgia tells of going shopping one day, and when she returned, the old man had pushed heavy boxes of the books out of their basement, onto the elevator and into their apartment, where he eventually autographed every one.

He says he worried that his lack of a college education would make his writing less significant, but then he decided, "Education doesn't help you understand right and wrong, only a good heart does."

Is he an evangelical? He chuckles. "No, no, no. Anything but. I understand that to mean fundamentalism, and, boy, I'm just the opposite. Everyone has their own God, but those fundamentalists want to make sure that theirs is mine. To me, God is your conscience. I read the Gospel of Matthew, and I got a sense of Jesus the social worker. That's what I'm looking for. But with all respect to Jesus, there are a lot of good religions, and a lot of good people who follow them.

"We all want to be better than we are, but in our society, it doesn't allow it. We're in a society that's dog-eat-dog. For example, if I'm going to sell you a used car, I should show you the bad parts, point out the bad transmission and the worn-down brakes. But if I do that, I get fired by the sales manager, and then my children don't eat. Right off, in society, I've got a morals mountain I can't climb.

"You can't survive in this corporate society and treat other people like you want to be treated. And I will go to my grave wishing I could have done more to change that."

Does he believe in an afterlife? "I don't know, but I guess not. I'm still trying to figure out this life," he says, then smiles. "Better hurry, huh?"

He does not want to die; he is afraid of dying. He is sad at the idea of not being. The question in his eyes is: "How can your lives be empty of me?"

The first week in December, the Wildfangs sign him up for hospice care. The hospice will deliver a portable hospital bed to their apartment when his time draws near, and offer counseling and other support. This represents the crossing of a bridge, because hospices only work with those who have less than six months to live.

Wildfang is unwavering in his determination to control his end, but he wants to square it with his children. So on a rainy night, he and Georgia drive to the house of his eldest son, Richard, where the children and their spouses await. They know about his disease and sense what he is thinking, but still. . . .They know what he has always wanted his life to represent, and although they all protest that they wouldn't mind taking care of him, there is no argument when he repeats several times that he wants to spare them an ordeal, and to also set an example of personal independence for others. Tears are blinked away because these are children trained in his own stoic culture, and they know he intends this to be his final social statement. "If that's what you want, Dad," they say over and over.

It is only when he speaks of their mother, Vivian, who had died so slowly decades earlier, that emotion breaks into tears, including his own wet eyes. "I really loved that gal," he says, speaking slowly, giving the words weight.

An old movie is playing on TV, and Georgia is out shopping on this wet and chilly afternoon in Salem. Wildfang feels talkative. He wanders among the years of his life, reliving the missions he undertook. He seems most proud of the years he spent pounding nails to build homes for the poor as a Habitat for Humanity volunteer. He also devoted decades fighting for small farmers in the National Farmers Union. And because he has a stepson and a great-granddaughter who are gay, he is active in Parents, Families and Friends of Lesbians and Gays.

"I've lived for almost a century, and I've still got the same big question I had when I was a boy: Most people want to do good, so why is it we can't make this earth work better? Why is poverty a price we're willing to pay for greed? In a short while I'm not going to be here anymore, and it won't be a long time after that all traces of me will disappear forever. Like I never existed. So what's it mean? I don't know, but then, fellows a lot smarter than me didn't know either." He pauses in counterpoint. "Looking back, I'm disappointed I couldn't make a bigger difference, but I guess I shouldn't overreach. I loved two good women, and raised four children who are a credit to me. On my last day, I'll have the thought that that's pretty good."

He says he doesn't put much stock in memorial services. "Too much about what people wish the life was about, not what it really was. I'd prefer that someone just read the list of things I've been involved with." He hands me a photocopy of a list written in a shaky hand. "This list is pretty much me."

Wildfang is enjoying a burst of strength, and the family takes advantage by observing an early Christmas on the 13th. About 30 relatives and four generations celebrate solemnly. Even the small children sense the gravity. The evening is loving, though a bit awkward. However, the timing is excellent because just the next day a new bout of pneumonia sets in.

The infection quickly drives Wildfang into a sickroom maintained by the retirement residence. In reality, it's a death-watch room, and he's aware of that. Wildfang says that he has three remaining tasks before he drinks the poison: He wants to distribute family memorabilia to his children, he wants to finish a letter-to-the-editor to the local newspaper on his political views, and he wants to wait until his final Social Security check has been mailed on Dec. 31 so that Georgia will have it, because they don't give money to dead men.

It's almost the end of the year now. Since Christmas, he has drifted in and out of grieving, as Rasmussen had predicted, and his spirits are being ground down. Finally, he tells Georgia he's ready to "do it." He leads her through a final discussion on the financial adjustments she'll have to make after he's gone. At one point, Wildfang's lifelong frugality surfaces in a way that gives Georgia a painful chuckle. He asks what will happen to the life-ending prescription if he ends up not drinking it, which Rasmussen told him is always a possibility. "I'll throw it away," she answers. Then, after saying that, and looking at his concerned expression, she realizes that his "waste-not" credo has instinctively kicked in, even on this.

* * *

On the 30th of December, in the middle of a snowstorm, it is decided. Tuesday, Jan. 6 will be the day, because Rasmussen is out of town until Jan. 5. The law doesn't require a physician's attendance, but Rasmussen wants to be at Wildfang's side. Georgia will pick up the prescription on Friday, Jan. 2, and have it filled the next day. Three days later, the family will gather at his and Georgia's home at an appointed hour. He will be wheeled from the infirmary to the elevator and up to their eighth-floor apartment. There, with the family gathered around, Rasmussen will mix the chemical into a drinkable solution and hand it to Wildfang. After saying his farewells, Wildfang will take his drink. He will have a few more moments with them, but with each minute he will grow more drowsy. After about five minutes, he will fall asleep. After about an hour, he will stop breathing.

While final plans are being made, his physical discomfort grows. It is Dec. 31, and his feet have developed a painful fungus, his tailbone is acutely sore, his breathing is more labored, and a yeast infection on his tongue resembles a huge strawberry because antibiotics have destroyed the "good" bacteria in his mouth. His body is breaking up. Even so, Wildfang is observing his final New Year's Eve knowing that his resolve has not failed him: The letter to the editor giving his antiwar views and a final swipe at corporate greed was published on the 28th, the Social Security check has been mailed today, and the plans to end his life are in place. Now he can rest and wait.

As on every day of this final ordeal, Georgia's morning begins and her evening ends at his side. Now, knowing that those days are being counted off one at a time, she is even more often with him.

On the very first morning of the new year, Georgia enters the room, approaches the bed and softly says, "Howard?" She says it again. A little louder, a little sharper. "Howard?" She doesn't say it again. Wildfang's illness has taken him. A final kiss.

Here is Howard l. Wildfang's list: National Farmers Union (69 years); PTA, local offices and state board of managers; Mid-Valley Community Action Program; Oregon Citizens Alliance; Interact; Habitat for Humanity; Polk County Historical Society; Neighbors Helping Neighbors; Heifer Project International; Christ's Church; Polk County and the City of Independence, Ore. (various offices); Oregon Farm Ministry; Parents, Families and Friends of Lesbians and Gays.

—Los Angeles Times Magazine, July 18, 2004

This 'soldier' went for service, not fortune

Derek Coleman treats a wounded Kurdish soldier.

Derek Coleman is a strapping, bright guy of 27 with a woodsman's beard who recently returned from going to see the elephant.*

In the Gold Rush of the mid-19th century, young fellows from the east would head for the Mother Lode [cq] country, and when asked why, they would say they were going to see the elephant.

Nobody knew exactly where that saying originated, but they all knew what it meant: exploring past the crest of the hill, finding out what the world offered.

The elephant coaxed Derek to Iraq and a lifetime of adventure squeezed into a year and a half.

* * *

Derek was just a guy of 25 a year and a half ago. He grew up mainly in San Marcos, California and loved being a machinist, certainly better than college where he had an unsatisfying cup of coffee. He had money in the bank and no attachments that tied him down.

"No kids that I know of, and no dog," he says.

He's an irreverent guy, whimsical, and penetrating in his judgments. He's thoughtful and well read. College didn't discourage that. He prefers BS to remain in the barnyard.

Derek also had a raging testosterone itch—he wanted adventure, and he wanted it now. However, an earlier head injury removed the military option, and he couldn't circumnavigate the globe in a hot air balloon.

"I was longing for some excitement. You know, this illogical thing that some men have where they just want to put themselves in danger." He shrugs. "I know, it doesn't make sense."

It hasn't made sense for thousands of years.

"Nobody learns the lesson of war, you know? It just kind of bounces right off your brain," he says.

"I read "For Whom the Bell Tolls" when I was in high school. It's about a man who volunteers for danger (the Spanish Civil War). I always thought that was an amazing thing for a man to give up his comfortable life in America and just go fight what he sees as evil." Another shrug. "I guess I've got delusions of grandeur."

Derek, you're a romantic.

"I guess. Yeah, for sure. Definitely."

What he didn't know he had was an impulse to risk his life to help the victims of war. He would discover that on the battlefields of Kurdistan.

Getting back to the itch: He had heard stories about volunteers going to Iraq to help the Kurds. He had no other offers, so...

"I sold pretty much everything I owned. I had a gun collection that helped fund it, and I sold my truck. I quit my job, which a lot of people thought I was crazy."

Derek, acting on the now-or-never throb of impulse, bought a ticket to Erbil, Kurdistan, the homeland of the Kurds, which is a grudging part of Iraq.

He soon found himself standing on that war zone tarmac in November 2015.

"Hello, Iraq. Here I am!"

* * *

Derek says, "Kurdistan is unique to the Middle East. Kurds are very open to other people's religions, other people's cultures. They're huge fans of Americans. If you say, 'I'm American,' they go, 'Oh, that's amazing.'

"Erbil's a pretty decent city. It's got restaurants and nice hotels, even a mall. You see women with hijabs and stuff, but you also see plenty of women who could be walking down a street here.

"Here's the thing. I mean, they're all Muslim, but they all drink. They break rules like anyone else."

Would the women date someone like you?

"No. No. It's a very conservative culture that way. I mean, I would kind of compare it to, like, early 1900s Western culture. "

Of course, too, every girl has a brother with an AK-47.

"Yeah. Exactly. I mean, you wouldn't want to risk it. There's a lot of Western women there. In fact, it's a great place to connect."

The Kurds have no affection for the rest of Iraq, except they and other Iraqis wallow in the same pool of oil. For the moment, though, they both are fighting ISIS; at least many Iraqis say they are, but the Kurds really are.

Why do the Kurds fight?

"Well, ISIS had taken some of their territory, and then they wanted to eliminate the Kurds. ISIS had no love for the Kurdish people, especially. I mean, ISIS might find allies in the Arabic world, but the Kurds are certainly not a part of their clique."

Derek's original idea was to fight, but no one offered him a rifle. The alternative was to join the thrown-together community of Western medical volunteers. Of course, he had no medical training, but he was there, so he switched to bandages and learned.

He was fortunate to buddy-up with a guy from New Jersey who was an EMT, and who taught him basic first aid which provided a platform to learn as he "practiced" in the real thing.

Derek's group was international, but the men who composed it were much like him—soldiers of fortune, but without guns and without pay. Guys in the group would come and go, ranging from a couple members up to a dozen. They ate with the military and scrounged medical supplies from richer groups such as the U.N. or aid detachments from various countries.

"We used our own money to buy a lot of stuff. If an oil company had a bunch of expired medical items, they'd say, 'Hey, do you guys want these?'

"We were always two days from running out."

He was a self-taught medic, but he was light years ahead of the Kurdish army, called the Peshmerga.

"The Perhmerga didn't have medics, and few doctors. Most of the soldiers there did not know how to put on a tourniquet. We'd hear about guys who get shot in the foot, then bleed out and die.

"Stabbed in the shoulder? Bleed out and die. They'd put the wounded in a truck, drive them to the nearest hospital; they're dead when they get there. There was literally zero treatment.

"So we trained Peshmerga fighters for months; over 1,000 in a three-day course. It was pretty intense. I mean, if you can teach somebody how to tie their bandana around an AK-47 cleaning rod to stop someone's bleeding, they've learned how to do a tourniquet."

Has that encouraged you to become a paramedic here at home?

"No. Different world. You know, 40 to 50 casualties a day with serious trauma, probably more than your average paramedic would see in years.

"They called me a doctor, which is funny: 'Doctor! Doctor!'"

How many days would you go between showers?

"Usually not more than two weeks, so it wasn't too bad. Very dusty and dirty, though. I'd have days where I'm kind of covered in other people's bodily fluids.

"It's the front line. It's a giant garbage heap. So even if I didn't shower for 10 days, I was not the worst smelling man. You've got thousands of soldiers just dumping things everywhere."

Including each other.

"Yeah. Yeah. Exactly. ISIS bodies would not be picked up. It was to show disrespect. There were a lot of wild dogs—huge animals—and there was a reason for that."

* * *

As the battle for nearby Mosul widened, the Peshmerga launched major attacks on ISIS in October of last year. Their primary aim was to recapture Kurdish villages close to Mosul, Derek says.

"Our plan (medical volunteers) was to be as close as possible to the fighting to where we could receive the casualties."

Were the Kurds good fighters?

"They were brave. They don't duck when people shoot at them. You can call them brave or stupid, I guess."

There are better ideas.

"Yeah, but it was quite entertaining. When they were ducking, then you knew that it was a bad situation. Like—okay, I definitely should be worried now."

How close were you to the front lines?

"Right there."

Derek describes the snap and crack of a bullet passing close by. "It's definitely a lot of laughs and joking around. I always used to say, 'It's fun, until it's not.'"

He quotes Churchill after first correcting my mangling of the passage: "'Nothing is so exhilarating as to be shot at without result.'

"What we'd do is we'd set up a (battlefield) location. We'd try to tell any officers that were nearby, and they would say, 'Okay, great. You do your thing.' We were basically the Kurdish military's medical (support) most of the time."

Did you talk to any ISIS prisoners?

"I mean, they don't speak English or maybe their guts are hanging out, so I never was able to kind of chat any up."

What did the Kurds do with prisoners?

"You would not want to be an ISIS prisoner. Any time they told me, 'Oh, that's an ISIS prisoner,' that was a dead man walking, in my mind."

What do the Kurds think of ISIS?

"I think most kind of realize it's just an ultra-fanatic sect. They see it as some kind of loonies within their own religion."

"Do Kurds and Iraqis like each other?"

"No. They are allies of convenience at this point. So I worry what will happen after the ISIS war's over. There's a lot of talk about a war between Kurdistan and (the rest of) Iraq."

What surprised you about war?

"War is mostly boring. It's a lot of sitting around, you know? Even some of the most intense battles, it's a lot of sitting around. It's exciting for 20 minutes and then it's nothing for three days.

"One thing I didn't really expect is how many children we would have to treat.

"ISIS has spent the last two and half years keeping other people out and keeping Mosul people in. Mosel was a population of a million trapped people. So people who tried to escape—old people, women and children—that was the most common way for civilians to get wounded."

The children. Derek hadn't counted on that.

* * *

Derek is a steely guy. His emotions are masked by an even tone and a straight-ahead gunfighter gaze. He spends words like a cheapskate does tips, but the things that happened to kids he can't let go of.

"There's one that haunts me the most. I ran up to the back of a Humvee and an entire family had been wounded; I think by a car bomb. There was a small boy who was dead and his brother was injured. So I climbed into the back to pick the wounded boy up.

"I put my arm behind his shoulders under his armpits. Then I put my other arm under his knees to carry him like you would. I didn't realize at the time that his legs were only attached by bits of skin. So when I picked him up, his legs actually slid out from my arm and I almost dropped him.

"His femur actually scraped my arm. He was screaming in my ear, and he's waving around, and his legs are flailing. I put him on the table and we started immediately treating him with tourniquets. Very quickly we loaded him into an ambulance. My clothes were covered in his blood."

What happened to the boy?

"He died a few minutes later." The shrug is in his voice. "What can you do?"

* * *

Derek spent a year instructing the Peshmerga (Kurdish) forces in basic battlefield first aid, and treating casualties of their battles with ISIS near Mosul. He and the other volunteers then found themselves out of work.

He says the Kurds backed off the fighting last November having achieved their objective of freeing Kurdish villages from ISIS.

Derek's group gravitated to the Iraqi army in its heavy fighting to free Mosul.

It was decision time for Derek and his friends. He says, "Do we go home? Do we join with the Iraqi army? We were very nervous about that because we had heard bad things about the Iraqis. They don't like Americans. We don't like them. We heard nobody was treating civilians, so we were, like—'Well, — it. Let's do it.'

"We just pulled up one day. We said, 'Hey. We're here to do medical for you.' There was one Iraqi officer who spoke a little English and he was just looking, like, 'Who are you guys? What is this?' They were standoffish."

Occasionally, Derek's group would run into U.S. military units that were there to advise and assist the Iraq army. He says with a grin, "I saw them 'advise and assist' the s— out of some ISIS fighters a couple of times.

"When we'd run into American units, they'd be amazed because we'd be driving our pickup trucks around. Of course, they'd be in giant vehicles that are 20 feet high and huge convoys and stuff. So, us running around saying, 'Hey, see you guys later. Thanks for the MREs,' (meals ready to eat) and we would just kind of drive away."

The volunteers threw themselves into the battle for Mosul. At one point, they were with units farthest into the city, knowing they would be prime targets for ISIS fighters wanting to deny medical help to their enemies.

The medics were treating up to 60 casualties per day; many were civilians, the flotsam of war.

Derek says, "Yeah. I mean, one bomb goes off to kill a soldier and there's 30 civilians nearby, you know? There's just simple math there."

He says about 25 percent of casualties were soldiers, 25 percent were children, and half were adult civilians.

"This is the way it would happen: A vehicle would pull up with injuries inside and we never knew what the cases were, or if it was, you know, a truck full of dead bodies, or a truck 'full' of one guy who broke his thumb."

Is life cheaper there? Does death simply have to be accepted?

"Yeah, it is. I met people who were my age who were young during the first Iraq war. They'd talk about having bombs go off right outside their schools, sometimes daily."

Derek would decompress his personal tension by trying to bandage spirits as well as limbs. "Every once in a while I'd buy a bag of candy and just hand it out. I'd hand out water to refugees and have them look like, you know, their faces would light up."

Doing little things when big things aren't around.

Derek says, "We dealt with lots of female injuries—bombs don't discriminate. There was a family that had a newborn baby. The woman was carrying the baby and the husband was carrying all their belongings. The woman looked terrified.

"They look at me as, you know, blonde hair, blonde beard, blue eyes, wondering who the hell I was. Once they realized I was there to help, I saw this kind of relief wash over them.

"We put her into the cab of this big truck and I handed her things up. She was just staring at me and smiling. I was smiling back at her. She started saying stuff, in Arabic, and our translator was like, 'Oh, she's saying you're an angel. Thank God you're here.'

"I'm standing at the bottom handing her, you know, a blanket, with a smile on my face....Yeah, that was cool. Every once in a while I needed a pick-me-up after some tough times there."

There was one time especially when Derek might have thought maybe going to Iraq was not a good idea.

"I ran to treat a wounded soldier and while we were loading him into a vehicle, people started running and driving away. A car bomb was (being driven) towards where I was. I just ran because I didn't know what to do.

"I remember I see this big armored vehicle going as fast as possible past me, driving away terrified, and I'm thinking—Okay, that thing's booking it as fast as it can and I'm on foot. I'm dead. There's no way I'm going to survive this. I'm just going to disappear any second now."

The bomb detonated, but he had gotten beyond the blast.

None of his group became a casualty during his time there, but that was because of luck, not lack of opportunity.

Do you have flashbacks?

"Yeah, injuries I've seen. Children that I've seen wounded or killed. So many burned people and people who were literally blown up. It smelled like burnt hamburger to me.

"I walk down the street and smell a restaurant, and it's like—Oh, wow. That reminds me of pulling out some charred dude, thinking he's alive, but he's not. It's weird. Very gory (images)."

How'd that change your view of war?

"How horrible it is. I didn't actually realize how many civilians are just destroyed by it."

* * *

Derek knew his time was winding down when the work his group was doing started to be smothered by bureaucracy, especially the UN and its World Health Organization. That's not what he signed up for.

"Someone like myself was not as needed anymore."

Bureaucracies give Derek a psychic itch, so in late April, he came home for good.

* * *

How did the experience change you?

"I don't know. It'll take a long time to see permanent effects. I'm more self-confident: 30 wounded people bleeding and screaming and it's my responsibility. I pleasantly surprised myself. Hey, even when I get shot at—I can cut it."

Derek says he went to Iraq with almost $10,000 cash, and came home owing about $6,000. That's an amount he calls "quite a bit." Everything was gone, spent on living expenses and medical supplies.

He says, "Not too bad for your average 27-year-old American with no college loan. However, I was never a penny in debt before I left for Iraq, so it weighs on me."

He plans to become an over-the-road trucker to repay his debts, but also—and perhaps more important—to roll down the window and feel the winds of the Great Plains on his face, and have his boss 1,000 miles away and out of cell phone reach.

How about police work? San Diego PD is looking for people.

"I'm actually a staunch Libertarian and so most police work to me would be bureaucratic."

A lot of life is.

"Yeah, and so I want to do my best to avoid that."

You're a lone wolf.

"Yeah, definitely. I don't like being put into a box. I kind of like to stay home. I don't go out on Friday nights and get wasted and this kind of thing because there's nothing crazy I really want to do anymore.

"I like helping people. I like the idea of conflict resolution."

Any thought of going back to school?

"No. I love to learn, but I hate school. I would always say I'd never let school get in the way of my education."

Derek has seen what weapons can do to flesh and bone, but he still loves his guns and hates bureaucracy—not a crowd-favorite combination for a Californian. To Derek, the line might be: If I can't carry, I won't tarry. Or something like that.

He plans to leave California soon, perhaps for Wyoming, Utah or Idaho where guns are household utensils.

There's no doubt in his voice when he says, "My goal is to be happy. I don't know how I'm going to do that, but I don't care how. I just know that's what I want."

* * *

There's a lot of throwback in Derek Coleman. And yes, I can see him in an earlier time; maybe as a cowboy; not the myth variety, but for real: a rootless Civil War veteran or a freed slave trying to find a place that fits.

He wouldn't be the trail-herd hand who jumps to the straw boss' orders, or would be content to choke in the dust of riding drag.

He'd be the lone fence rider, spending his days repairing barbed wire and rescuing calves from mud holes.

He'd have a pistol in his bedroll, but only rattlesnakes would need worry.

("Going to see the elephant" most likely originated from excited rustics of the mid-1800s traveling to see a road-show circus and its near-mythic elephant—a big adventure.)*

San Diego Union-Tribune, June 12 & 19, 2017

Life I've observed along the way

Where hope survives like a buried seed

I've never cared for the word "ghetto." It seems a put-down of good people forced by circumstance into a bounded living space.

But the word fits like no other for an area of San Diego just south of downtown along I-5 and east on Imperial Avenue. It's a ghetto of dire circumstance that remains largely hidden because most of us avoid seeing it.

If old-industrial Ohio is the rust belt, then this is the grim belt. Welfare agencies are the only growth industry. There is no grass here; even the weeds seem stressed. Midday, the traffic is light and then largely of trucks that pass on through, watchful black and whites, and tired autos scarred by the dent-wounds of a long life.

Along the streets are people from whom we avert our eyes. They are mostly men, often with scruffy, graying beards pushing purloined grocery carts or carrying large plastic bags over their shoulders. Adrift on a river with no name. They don't appear to speak, even in their clusters that gather in the corners of parking lots. There's not a lot to talk about. Obamacare? What does that have to do with me? The Chargers? Are you serious?

They already know where the meals and beds can be found. Any casual comment might ignite a rambling tirade from someone off his meds and whose mind is traveling somewhere off the coast of Saturn.

The few women tend to be younger, and not by accident. Living on the streets is not a place for a woman to grow old. Things happen. The women we see tend to keep walking, en route to a seedy apartment, or perhaps to see the fellow who sells the meth, or maybe a step behind some guy they should run from like a plague carrier.

There are no children visible, and if there were, they wouldn't be playing.

There is no reminder that this is the holiday season, until…in a small front window of a shabby, tiny house something is written, facing outward, scrolled free-hand with what looks like soap. It says—"Happy Holidays."

But it says more. It says: "I am here, such as I am, and I want to be happy, too."

In a paved lot at the corner of 16th Avenue and Newton Street, there is a large circus-size tent. It's the San Diego Winter Shelter Program for the homeless operated by the Alpha Project, one of the charities that actually grabs a shovel and does heavy labor serving the unbeautiful and the poor.

The tent looks like a refugee center thrown up to shelter victims of some hellacious storm. This is turbulence not seen on the weather report. It is often a hiding place from hunger and cold; a warehouse filled with people and crowded with hopelessness.

Inside, the tent is organized along rows of bunks, some stacked two high. Men are at one end, women at the other; also separated are husbands and wives. And that line is not crossed. Security is tight and no-nonsense. There are no children. The bunks are piled high with plastic-bag luggage holding the essentials for surviving in their Kalahari, and perhaps a few keepsakes from a better life. To many, the term "new year" is empty of promise, bereft of hope.

Through it all, some are fighting against the mud that traps their feet, and are intent on reversing their condition by effort and attitude.

The wise Viktor Frankl wrote: "The last of (our) freedoms is to choose one's attitude in any circumstance."

The clinging web that traps the addict

Here's the thing about heroin—it's wonderful. Nothing like it in the world. The Brahms Lullaby caresses your brain, and your blood is warm nectar. The world is perfect and you are perfect in it.

Heroin is pleased to be the love of your life. All it requires is that you steal from your children, reject your mate, forsake your family, and abandon your career. Then, of course, you will be expected to spend your days in the gutter or prison. To earn its favor you have to pledge suicide when it asks. And it will.

If you attempt to break away, its smile will be knowing. "Remember who loves you," it will say. "I'll be here for you."

Thoughts about an achieving Hispanic teenager

I've never liked the statement, "She (or he) is a credit to her race." It implies that such "credit" is unexpected, rare, or sort of hyphenated, either to her or the race. It's the type of mentality that plays into themes of both the race-baiters and race-hustlers. Melissa Palafox is a credit to herself.

Though she is respectful toward her parents' roots and her own heritage, Melissa has been to Mexico only once, when she was 2 years old.

This is as Americanized a girl as any cheerleader in Iowa.

The credit she has earned is shared by a society that has delivered on its promise to help Melissa grow tall; to her father who gets down on his knees to pull weeds for her; to her mother who cleans others' toilets for her; but mainly to the girl herself who has brushed aside the grasping hands of defeatism, and by hard work has cultivated a field where promise can flower.

As I take my leave...

As I've said at the end of all my columns—Every life is an adventure. I believe these stories affirm that truth. I thank every 'adventurer' portrayed in this book, and also you: may all your adventures unfold under a warm sun.